What people are sa

CW00506341

# Self-Love Pl

*Self-Love Pledge* touched me so deeply. It's so authentic, real, and true – a book that's definitely needed for today. This is a book about falling back in love with ourselves. I believe we are born loving ourselves, but things happen and get in our way. This is something that can really help people return to that place of self-love. *Self-Love Pledge* is beautiful; absolutely beautiful.
**Theresa Cheung**

*Self-Love Pledge* is honest, deeply vulnerable, and practical. Through her heart-warming stories Katie Oman captures the true essence of self-love, and teaches us how to be unapologetically ourselves.
**George Lizos**, Spiritual Teacher

## Reviews

I don't even know where to start with this book! With how brave and genuine you are. What an incredible writer you are. How I cry and feel with you for your journey. And how excited I am for your new chapters to come.
I love your book! Simple as that!
It's easy to read, clear, authentic and with lots of great practical suggestions too.
**Eva Wisenbeck**

Your book is really authentic and I can actually hear your lovely voice coming through as I read it. I think the authenticity is really important. Secondly, it's really open. You share your experiences, and exactly how they made you feel, and how you dealt with them. I think a lot of people will connect with that; there is something there for everyone. Keep being you! I know this book will help so many people.

**Gemma Sandwell**

# Self-Love Pledge

How Learning to Love Myself Led to
True Happiness

# Self-Love Pledge

## How Learning to Love Myself Led to True Happiness

### Katie Oman

BOOKS

Winchester, UK
Washington, USA

**JOHN HUNT PUBLISHING**

First published by O-Books, 2019
O-Books is an imprint of John Hunt Publishing Ltd., 3 East St., Alresford,
Hampshire SO24 9EE, UK
office@jhpbooks.com
www.johnhuntpublishing.com
www.o-books.com

For distributor details and how to order please visit the 'Ordering' section on our website.

ISBN: 978 1 78904 337 2
978 1 78904 338 9 (ebook)
Library of Congress Control Number: 2019931138

A CIP catalogue record for this book is available from the British Library.

Design: Stuart Davies

UK: Printed and bound by CPI Group (UK) Ltd, Croydon, CR0 4YY
US: Printed and bound by Thomson-Shore, 7300 West Joy Road, Dexter, MI 48130

We operate a distinctive and ethical publishing philosophy in
all areas of our business, from our global network of authors to
production and worldwide distribution.

# Contents

You yourself, as much as anybody in the entire universe, deserve your love and affection.
– *Buddha*

*You have been criticizing yourself for years, and it hasn't worked. Try approving of yourself and see what happens.*
– *Louise L. Hay*

*I was once afraid of people saying, 'Who does she think she is?' Now I have the courage to stand and say, 'This is who I am.'*
– *Oprah Winfrey*

For the people that have helped me come home to myself through their unconditional love: my mum, my children, and Theresa Cheung.

# Prologue

*'Enough! Help me, please!'*

My balled-up fists struck the carpet underneath me as the tears poured down my face. I was broken, lost, and oh so tired. It felt as though I'd been struggling for years, like an oarsman trying to row against the tide. To everyone else it may have looked as though I'd been slowly moving forwards, but it was getting harder and harder to keep going with the way things were. How could they when the very boat itself was disintegrating around me?

The year was 2016. I was living within a marriage that was broken beyond repair, but I could see no way out of it. We were living hand to mouth every single day, and the belts around our household were getting so tight they were running out of notches. Every time I went to the cash machine, I prayed that it would give me money, and more times than not I was greeted with the words *'insufficient funds'*. With three children to look after, my worry tower was crumbling around me, and I was terrified. Desperate for change, but deep in fear that things might become even worse than they were already if I attempted to change things – I was frozen.

Stuck but scared.

Couldn't move forwards.

Couldn't stay where I was.

I was at the end of my tether but had no clue which way to turn.

Despite being surrounded by love from my parents, friends and children, I felt desperately alone in that moment. Even though I have been spiritually awakened since 2010, I was even losing my way on that path. I truly felt as though I was a separate, lost and alone person. I felt as though I had created this hopeless mess, and yet could see no way back to the light.

1

It is said that in our darkest moments, most people call upon a power greater than themselves. Despite my spiritual teachings and inspirational words to others, I had not done the one thing that would've brought me guidance, love and support: I hadn't asked for help. I was carrying the weight of everything on my shoulders, and I was rapidly running out of strength and energy.

Now, as my body shook with desperate sobs, I practically screamed my heart out, *'Help me, please! I can't do this anymore!'*

Silence.

And then, ever so softly, quietly, gently, my heart swelled inside my chest. I felt it grow and burst open; an overwhelming feeling of love pouring out like a cool refreshing rain after a long drought. This love rapidly filled my being. Every cell of my body, and even the spaces in-between the cells, was filled with the glorious light of love.

My tears stopped, and I took a deep breath right down into my stomach. That's when I heard it – a whisper on the breeze:

*'It's time to love yourself.'*

# Introduction

For as long as I can remember I have wanted to be someone else.

Not only that, but I made friends with girls who had all the qualities I wished to have for myself.

There was Natalie, the adventurous and spirited girl.

Lisa, the graceful and creative girl.

Laura, the fiery and powerful girl.

I seemed to make friends with people who I would've swapped places with in a heartbeat. In them, I saw all the qualities that I believed were lacking in myself. Whenever I stopped to consider who I was and compared myself to these friends, I always saw myself as lacking in some way. Less than them. I certainly wasn't loving myself in any way at all.

There was no logical reason for this crooked mindset. I was born as the only child to two loving parents, and was given an endless supply of love, opportunity and abundance as I grew older. Yes, my parents got divorced when I was eight years of age, but they made it crystal clear that they still both loved me dearly and did all they could to put my needs first. I was consistently told how amazing, beautiful and clever I was. My self-confidence was forever being boosted and, to the outside world, I should've been a girl who truly loved and believed in herself.

And yet...

I never thought of myself with loving thoughts. When I looked in a mirror, I only saw the parts of myself that I didn't like, not even noticing anything positive about myself at all. In my eyes, I was a person who was different, awkward, and not as good as those around me. Even now, as I write these words, I feel a deep sense of sadness in my heart. It's not an easy thing to admit to you, but I know it's important to strip myself back and show my truth. In that way I can really try to help all those who feel the way I did.

I felt this way for approximately 34 years of my life. The very concept of loving myself was totally alien to me. I mean, I barely liked who I was most of the time, so there was little chance of giving myself the actual love I so desperately needed. Not loving or accepting myself for who I was placed me in some situations that were really not good for me (more on that later), but I never understood my part in it. Instead, I was the perpetual victim of circumstance and other people's behaviour. The notion that my opinion of myself was colouring my world to such an extreme degree went completely over my head.

*Low self-esteem is like driving through life with your hand brake on.*
*– Maxwell Maltz*

As I sat on my bedroom floor that night, the tears drying on my blotchy face, my eyes widened in surprise.

Of course! It was all so bloody obvious now!

Up until that point, I had never had an out-of-body experience but, in that moment, I saw myself as an objective outsider. I saw the hurt and frightened young girl inside me longing to be loved. I saw all the good things I had put into the world, and all the people whose lives I had touched. I saw my huge heart, my faith in the innate goodness of people, and my ever-ready smile.

As fresh tears sprang to my eyes, I smiled in a deep realisation: I am okay just as I am. More than that – I am a wonderful person and I deserve to love myself. I had no idea how this understanding would help me make my home life better, but there was an unshakeable feeling that I had just taken a very important step in the right direction. Learning to love myself was going to be the magical key that would unlock the door to a happier future.

The past two years have seen me on a journey of self-love, growth and transformation like no other that I have ever experienced before. I have gone from pain to happiness; from fear to love. I truly have gone from zero to becoming my own hero.

And you can too! The more I have posted on social media about loving yourself, the more I have come to the realisation that so many people don't like the person they are. Just like I was two years ago, so many people are finding it hard to accept themselves for who they are, or to give themselves any kind of love or care. And, just like I had experienced, these beliefs are leaving negative footprints all over their lives.

That's why I wanted to write this book. My previous book, *Happiness: Make Your Soul Smile*, was written because I saw that a lot of people were struggling with the concept of how to be happy. In the same vein, I now see that many people not only don't love themselves, but don't even know how to start that journey. Throughout this book, I will take you on the journey I have been on. I will share everything I have learned and experienced with you in that time. My hope is that, through reading my words, your heart will also crack open with love for yourself, as mine did on that bedroom floor. That you will be able to truly see and understand yourself like never before, and comprehend why learning to love yourself is one of the greatest gifts you can give to yourself.

Come on this journey with me now. You have taken the most important step by simply picking up this book. It's time to welcome love into your life with an open mind and an open heart.

# What is Self-Love Anyway?

You may have picked up this book and are now worried what people may think of you if they see you reading it. After all, there is still a misconception amongst some people that self-love is somehow a sign of narcissism or vanity.

*'You're a bit full of yourself, aren't you?'*
*'Oh, my goodness! Ego or what!'*
*'How big-headed are you?'*

To say these people are missing the point would be the understatement of the year! Don't get me wrong, there are certain individuals that will take self-love to that place. In every practice, there are those who bring the ideas and methods to a more negative space, but any kind of narcissism couldn't be further removed than what I'm talking about in this book.

So, if we're not going to focus on vanity, what exactly *is* self-love? Well, in a nutshell, self-love means accepting and appreciating yourself for who you are! You celebrate the true uniqueness that is you, and understand the value of all you have to contribute in life. That means never feeling the need to apologise for simply being yourself, and not allowing yourself to settle for less than you deserve, and to know categorically that you always deserve to be treated with love and respect. Ultimately, the main goal of self-love is to live a life that allows you to be mentally, emotionally, physically and spiritually happy and healthy.

*Loving yourself... does not mean being self-absorbed or narcissistic,*
*or disregarding others. Rather it means welcoming yourself as the*
*most honoured guest in your own heart, a guest worthy of respect,*

*a loveable companion.*

*– Margot Anand*

Sound good?

When you break the concept down to what it truly means, you start to understand that this is something you need in your life, and how could anyone *not* want to feel that way? Simply put, learning to love yourself is the foundation of happiness, but that doesn't mean that it's the easiest thing to bring into your life.

When we are babies, our light shines so brightly, without any kind of fear or self-doubt. Infants accept themselves totally as they are; they are pure love in essence! But, as we grow older and have to go out into the world, we start to experience things and other people that may put huge dampeners on our ability to love and accept ourselves in this way.

As I said before, there was no logical reason for me to not like or accept the person I am... at first. Like many people, the first time I truly experienced others who didn't like me was at school. Combine this with the normal doubts and angst of being a teenager, and I was in real trouble! I was already feeling different from those around me when I entered my high school at 12 years of age. Although I have always appeared as a smiley, bubbly, extroverted person on the outside, inside I was a turbulent mix of doubts and anxiety. Indeed, my vivacious personality became to some degree a tactic; a mask. I genuinely thought that if I could make people laugh, that they would like me and I would fit in. For a teenager, fitting in is everything, and I was desperate to feel as though I was liked and accepted.

You can't change the past of course, and I do believe that everything happens for a reason, however, I can't help but wonder what the outcome might have been had I gone to a mixed-sex school. Would I have had an easier and more joyful school experience? Perhaps, perhaps not, and that's something

I'll never know. All I do know is that my secondary school education was spent at an all-girls grammar school, and this has left a bigger mark on me than I ever could have realised.

Single-sex schools may be seen as being a good thing by some. Surely, without the distraction of the other gender, students can achieve more and get better grades? I have no way of knowing if this is the case for boys schools of course, but, in my experience, nothing could be further from the truth for an all-girls school!

My time spent at that grammar school was a time of bullying, anxiety and an awful lot of unhappiness. Not every second of every day, of course. I did have a group of friends and many a happy moment, but the overriding focus of that part of my life was torment. I realise now that the behaviour of those girls who bullied me spoke volumes about their own issues, but when you're a teenager you don't stop to consider this. In your head, the fact that people don't like you is clearly your own fault. If only you were cooler/funnier/prettier/more like them they would stop picking on you and magically start being your friend.

Being a teenager is basically a red flag to your own neurosis and issues. What may have started as a niggling feeling that I was different from those around me became a raging volcano in the face of that time. Being the target for people's mental and emotional abuse over a long period is bound to leave an impact on you. I see now it was that time that truly plunged my self-worth and self-esteem into the pit of loathing. After all, the mind is merely a computer that functions according to whatever you program into it. What you continuously focus on is what it accepts as true, even if those messages come from people around you.

My internal operating system was running the **'Hate Yourself'** program on loop, and I was totally oblivious to the fact that I had the power to change it; we all do! If my words so far have rung all too true for you, and you see yourself echoed in me, know that it doesn't have to be this way! You do have a choice about how you see yourself. It isn't the case that some people are born loving themselves and the rest of us are doomed into the self-loathing pit (no matter how true that may feel). Every single one of us has a choice.

Peel back the layers of who you are. Who are you really?

You may start with your job or role as a parent, spouse, or child.

Peel it back further. What do you see now?

Your age perhaps? Or your gender?

Keep peeling back the layers of all your labels and identities that you see yourself as, all the way down to your core; the true essence that is you. Who are you?

## LOVE

You are love. You come from love, you are made from love, and to love you will return. Away from the constructs, the roles, and the identities, love is who you really are. And you spend the vast amount of your life looking to give this love away, and for other people to give their love to you. You seek validation, worth, and confidence through the love of another, and yet that has the potential to place you in dangerous territory.

No matter who that person is, they can be taken away from you. Relationships crumble every single day. If you only look for love from others, what will happen if you find yourself suddenly alone? Does this now take away all that validation and worth that you found through them loving you? There is nothing wrong with letting people love you, of course; love is our main purpose in life. But, it doesn't mean that this has to be your one-stop shop for bringing love into your life. There is another way.

When you seek to love yourself first, then you have a bedrock that'll be with you, regardless of whether anyone else is loving you or not. You won't seek any sense of worth or validation through another because you understand that you can give it to yourself. It's like filling up your own cup first before you allow anyone else into your space. When they give their love to you, you can then accept it because you want to, rather than from any desperate sense of needing it.

So, what are the issues of not loving yourself? After all, many people really struggle with this, so surely it can't be that damaging, right? Sadly, for me at least, it proved to be very damaging indeed.

The girls at high school continued to bully me for the entirety of my time there. Like all bullying scenarios, some days were better than others, but it never truly stopped completely. Writing this book has made many memories from that part of my life rise up inside my mind, but there's one in particular that haunts me the most. Being the time period that this was (mid-90s), there were no mobile phones, and I had no need to take money with me to school. Consequently, I used to leave my school bag in the classroom during lunch break whilst I went to get my food; most of us did. It was never something that you found yourself debating, and it had certainly never been an issue in the past. Not until one day when I was 14, that is.

As I came back to the classroom, I became instantly aware that something was different. One of the girls who had been bullying me was poking her head out of the door on lookout. Spotting me, she darted back into the room and I heard a muffled giggling pouring out from behind the door. I felt the dread rise up in my throat as I pushed the classroom door open, worried about what I might find on the other side. The first thing I noticed was that the only girls in the room were those who had been tormenting me. Lunch break hadn't finished yet and most of the other students were still downstairs. Their faces leered at me, full of smug sneers and pride at what they had done.

What had they done?

Emptied the contents of my school bag all over the floor for a start. My books and pens were scattered, as was my hairbrush and sanitary pads. They seemed to take the greatest pleasure in strewing out my pads the most, for each one had been placed in different places; including one on the teacher's desk. The bag itself was nowhere to be seen and was later found in the girl's toilet, wedged down the side of one of the toilets. Written across the whiteboard in large letters were the words, 'Kate is a slag'. The tears stung my eyes as their cruel laughter rang in my ears. Like every other incident, however, I didn't tell anyone who would've had the power to help me. In my mind, telling would be a huge red flag to them and the bullying would get even worse. I honestly believed that if I ignored it and acted as if they weren't getting to me then they would get bored and stop. They didn't.

By the time I had completed my GCSEs I had experienced their nastiness for nearly four years, and my self-esteem was on the floor. Their cruel jokes and torments had fully lodged themselves in my brain and had become my truth. I truly believed all of the things they said about me and never stopped to consider the possibility that I could be anything else. Even getting good grades in my exams wasn't enough to make me open my eyes to my own potential.

The brain believes whatever you or anyone else consistently tells it. Four years of being told that you're stupid, ugly, and worthless nearly every day would be enough to make even the most confident of people start to doubt themselves. Like a character in a classic cartoon, I felt as though I permanently had an angel on one shoulder and a devil on the other. On the one side was my mum telling me that I was so clever and capable. On the other were the bullies calling me thick and worthless. The trouble was, their voices were louder.

In fact, so low was the depth of my own sense of worth and esteem that the thought of ending it all seriously crossed my mind. Those girls' voices at school had become my inner dialogue; a ticker tape of hate that shouted through my head 24/7. Aged 16, I was tired. Tired of the bullying, the fear, the wishing to be someone else. I honestly started to believe that things would be better if I just slipped quietly away, or even if I had never been born at all. I would stare at the tablets in the cabinet, wondering what it would be like to take them all. Or, I'd fantasise about stepping out into oncoming traffic. Writing these things now makes me desperately sad for that young woman who felt so lost, and I wish I could travel back and wrap my arms around her. It's so sad that I allowed those girls to push me down that far. The thought of what may have happened had I been braver makes me shudder. Because, ultimately, that was the reason I didn't go through with ending things: I was too scared to. Frightened that it may hurt, scared that it would work, worried that it wouldn't. Terrified of the impact it would have on my parents and family. No, I couldn't work up the courage to permanently stop the bullying once and for all, but it was crystal clear that I had to get away from my tormentors. I couldn't risk staying and have the possibility of making such a drastic decision become more of a reality in my life.

So, despite my passion for English, and my secret dreams of being a writer, I bailed. I was more than capable of staying on and doing my A Levels, but I simply couldn't face being around the nasty girls for a second longer. At 16, the careers advisor came into school to help us decide what we wanted to do after our exams. A tightly-wound woman with a clipboard and a checklist, she looked personally insulted when I meekly stated that I didn't know what I wanted to do with my life. A crimson rash crept up her neck and she anxiously asked me if I had any part-time jobs or work experience that I could pursue. Ten minutes later, I was back outside in the blinding winter sun, clutching a prospectus for a college I didn't really want to go to, so that I could study a course I wasn't passionate about, and wondering what the hell had happened. Because of my own lack of self-belief and worth, I found myself studying something that I wasn't particularly interested in for the next two years of my life: childcare. In fact, for the first year of the course I barely did any work at all and had to literally do nearly two years' worth of work in one. I passed... just.

Not once did I stop and say, *'Erm, excuse me? I don't really want to be a nursery nurse. I want to be a writer instead.'* Because, at that point in time, I honestly didn't believe for one second that I **could** be a writer! My dreams were going completely unfulfilled and I was miserable, and yet I didn't have the belief in myself to do anything about it. In fact, it would take me another fourteen years to finally allow myself to follow my passions and make those dreams come true.

How I wish I could say that not loving yourself only meant that you don't allow yourself to follow your dreams. If this was the only negative effect, solving it would be relatively straightforward. But, not loving yourself has an impact that has far more wide-reaching consequences than just that. Consequences that can cripple you for years to come because it affects the kind of people you bring into your life. Especially ones that are focused on love and sex.

Not loving yourself is a sure-fire way to lead you down a path of unhappiness in this department. You may as well be carrying a giant neon sign above your head that says, **'Only abusers, liars, cheaters and weirdos may apply.'** It's as if you have some vibe about you that only they can sense, and these people are attracted to you like a magnet. It may feel very unfair. After all, you're struggling to love and accept yourself. Why can't you bring someone else in who can help you with it? Don't you deserve better?

Yes, you really do deserve better (*so* much better!), but the people you are drawing into your life are a mirror, reflecting back at you how you feel about yourself. It's like watching all your neuroses, anxieties, and issues walking around in front of you. What makes this situation even more seemingly hopeless is the fact that many people who don't love themselves will actually put up with this bad behaviour from others because they don't really believe that they deserve any better. And I'm not blaming you when I say that; I simply want you to see your part in it all, for when you start to understand that then you have a greater power to turn things around and make them better for yourself.

*If you aren't good at loving yourself, you will have a difficult time loving anyone, since you'll resent the time and energy you give another person that you aren't even giving to yourself.*
*– Barbara De Angelis*

The things I talk about aren't merely hypothetical scenarios that I've read about in some self-help book; they have been my reality for many years. My dating history reads like a who's who of men that were no good for me. Whether it was issues with anger; not being able to move on from the past so they carried around like a perpetual victim; or chronic lying, it feels as though I've had more than my fair share of unhealthy relationships. And yes, I was totally oblivious to my part in it all. I mean *oblivious*. Not only did I complain to anyone who would listen that I could never meet anyone who respected me and treated me like I deserved to be treated, but I actually believed that if only I could love them hard enough that I could help them to be better.

(Sigh.)

Let me give you an example.

I dated a man (let's call him Robert) for two years. If I could go back in time and give myself a kick up the butt about this guy, believe me I would in a heartbeat. Even when I first got together with Robert, I knew he wasn't the kind of man that seemed to be a good fit for me. Indeed, when I met him, he was homeless, sleeping on a friend's sofa, and working in a low-income job. He smoked like a chimney, had been in trouble at school for his anger issues, and didn't really get on with some key members of his family. Many alarm bells should have been ringing, but I honestly thought I could help him. More than that, I was bloody *grateful* that he liked me!

Yes, grateful! Such were the depths of my self-loathing, I never stopped to consider if any man I dated was good or right for me, or even if I really liked them. For years, I was always surprised when I found out that any guy was attracted to me, and I would jump in head first before anyone had a chance to say, *'Wake up, Katie, and smell the issues!'*

I did eventually walk away from Robert, but not until things had gotten so bad that I couldn't deny the mountain of problems in our relationship to myself any longer. This was a man who emotionally and mentally abused me. Such was the depth of his own insecurities that he gently eroded any sense of worth I had over those two years; chipping at it until there was barely anything left. He cut me off from my friends and was constantly suspicious and paranoid that I would cheat on him with another man. A man who threw a wall clock at my head when I asked him to help me tidy up, missing my head by mere millimetres. A man who would hit me in his sleep and claim to have no recollection of it in the morning... night after night. A man who told me I couldn't wear certain clothes or make-up because they made me look like a whore.

Recently, I found a letter I had written to my mum when I was 19. You see, I had actually left Robert three months previous to writing this letter. It had become undeniable that his anger was a third party in our relationship, and I was starting to get really worried about being with him. However, he didn't take the news of our break-up well, and actually started to stalk me in an attempt to make me feel sorry for him and go back to him. During my part-time job as a sales attendant at a local petrol station, he would literally stand over the road during my shifts and watch me as I worked. The final straw came when he burst into my work in floods of tears, begging me literally on his knees to give him a second chance. He promised that he would get help for his anger issues and that things would be different between us. Believing myself to be in love with him, I agreed to try again, but I was worried about telling my parents. I had criticised him loads to them since our break-up, and I was anxious about what they might say, so I started to see him in secret.

After a couple of months, Robert convinced me to leave home and move into his bedsit with him. So, whilst my parents were both at work, I packed a bag and left. Worse than this though is the fact that I didn't speak to them for three days. They had no knowledge where I was, or even if I was okay. As a mother myself now, I can only begin to imagine the worry and heartache they must have gone through at that time. On the third day, I wrote the letter, trying to explain to them why I did what I did. Reading it now makes me ashamed and deeply embarrassed... especially because not all the words are mine. I did write them a letter, but Robert said he would fax it over to them from work. The letter I wrote was not exactly the letter they got, but I didn't know that at the time.

Robert went on to further control and abuse me both emotionally and mentally for another 18 months. This whole situation with me leaving home and writing them a letter should have been a huge red flag to wake me up and see the depth of Robert's issues, but I was deep in denial mode. I allowed him to treat me the way he did, and made excuses for him time and time again. I was convinced that it was nothing less than what I deserved and was absolutely terrified of the idea of being on my own. Being in the relationship broke me down so much that I ended up a husk of a woman who couldn't see the truth of the man she was with and, even if I had, I would've told myself that things weren't so bad; such was the poor quality of the relationship I had with myself at that point.

Thank goodness I had my mum and stepdad to help remove me from that toxic situation. Such was the powerful effect his constant put-downs and power games had on me that I'm not sure I would've had the strength to leave that relationship without them.

This situation wouldn't be so awful if I could confidently tell you that I learnt my lessons from it, and never put myself in circumstances like that again; but we both know that's not true. Time and time again, I kept placing myself in situations with controlling men who used their power to abuse and dominate me. In all honesty, it's only now at 36 that I finally get it. I see now that each relationship I've had was a perfect mirror to how I felt about myself. That if I had spent more time looking to love, nurture and care for myself, then I would've been less likely to have been so desperate to give my love away to the first man that came along. It's only now that I have learned how to truly love and accept myself for who I am, and I understand that I do deserve a relationship that brings me respect and real love. I'm not willing to accept anything less. When you know your worth, the game changes.

It's worth pointing out that this kind of situation doesn't only have romantic love as its foundation. Friendships, work colleagues, family, even acquaintances – **every** relationship you're experiencing right now is a clear reflection of how you feel about yourself. And, it's not until you learn how to love yourself that you are better able to bring in the right people who will treat you as you deserve to be treated: with love, respect, understanding, and compassion. Anything less than that isn't worth your time or your energy.

I hope you have a better understanding of what loving yourself means, and the powerful effect it can have on your life. It is one of the most beautiful and powerful gifts we can give ourselves. It is the gateway to happiness.

# Starting the Journey

Back to the bedroom floor.

When we last saw me there, my heart had been cracked open with love for myself after I had begged for help. The flood of tears that had only moments ago been pouring down my face had been replaced with the biggest smile. I didn't know what was going to happen next or how things were going to work out, but I did know one thing: I was going to be okay. Whatever did happen next, I wasn't going to smash into a million pieces, nor fall into an infinite darkness that I couldn't get out of. I was strong and more than capable; I knew it in that moment like I had never known before.

End of journey, right?

That's it then. Katie loves herself, all is good with the world, and you may as well put this book back on the shelf.

HAHAHA!

Come on now! You know that's not how it goes!

How many of you have tried to quit smoking/lose weight/ exercise, or any other new habit? Did you succeed the first time around and never have to worry about it ever again?

If you did, I'm literally taking my hat off to you. You are amazing, don't ever forget that!

But, for the majority of us, that's not how the story goes. Just because you have a truckload of good intentions at first doesn't mean that the process of change is easy or straightforward. Most of us have to go through the revolving door a few times before the change becomes a permanent fixture in our lives. I know I certainly did!

The day after the night before, I woke up bouncier and happier than I had been in a very long time. I was full of a new zest for life, and in that moment, I had more love for myself than I had in all the other 34 years of my life combined. I was invincible, titanium, and I honestly felt as though nothing could topple me from that pedestal ever again. Then life came in and gave me a push off my perch. That day, I experienced the following:

- I shouted at my children through my own stress levels = guilt.
- My work trousers were a bit tight on me = felt fat and ugly.
- I heard some colleagues giggling, but all fell silent when I walked in = paranoia that they all secretly hate me.
- Ate a piece of cake = felt like a greedy cow with no self-control.
- Looked in the mirror and saw a very tired woman looking back at me who I didn't recognise = felt very sorry for myself and hopeless.
- Cut my hand = felt like a clumsy oaf and clearly crap at my job.

Voila! From a love-filled bubble of happiness to my self-esteem back on the floor, and all in the space of six hours! And, why is this? How could my good intentions magically disappear so quickly?

When you start to try and love yourself, you'll find yourself up against a few things. First off, you are dealing with *years* of beliefs about how awful you have told yourself you are. It's like going to deep clean an old house that has been left untouched for years and only opening all the windows. You can't be surprised when the layers of dust and dirt are all still there; you haven't even begun to touch them! Like ingrained muck, low self-esteem and a low sense of self-worth don't magically dissolve overnight, no matter how many good intentions you may have.

*Most of the shadows in life are caused by standing in one's own sunshine.*
*— Ralph Waldo Emerson*

Secondly, the intention isn't enough. Don't get me wrong – *wanting* to change is a huge step, and actually the most important one. Nothing is going to get better unless you actually *want* it to, but it's not enough on its own. To make real and long-lasting changes, you need to have a toolbox of things that you can refer to time and time again. And this is what this book is for. Yes, I want to help you understand what self-love is and why it's so important, but I'm not just going to tell you my story and then leave you to figure the rest out by yourself. Going on this journey can be difficult enough without me not trying to signpost the way.

By the time I got home that afternoon, my opinion of myself was on the floor. I had 'failed' before I had even got going. Who was I to even try and love myself anyway? Clearly, I was so crap that I couldn't even do that right! I went up to my bedroom with heavy feet and looked at myself in the mirror. No words left my lips. I simply sat there and looked at myself. Who knew how long I stayed in that position? Five minutes, maybe half an hour, but as I truly looked at myself, a shift started to happen within me. Although not a word left my mouth, my brain was relentless:

*'You're crap.'*
*'You're useless.'*
*'You can't do anything right.'*
*'You fail at everything.'*

On and on and on. All my metaphorical dirt of self-loathing kicked up to the surface, and it was relentless. For a moment, I almost gave up. The onslaught was so vicious and unrelenting that I could literally feel myself falling into a pit of hatred that would be deeper than anything I had ever experienced before.

At this point, I would normally flee from my reflection and try to distract myself with another task, although my mind would still be on the merry-go-round of negativity. But, this time was different. It was as if I was physically unable to tear my gaze away from the glass. And, the more I looked, the more I could feel something shifting inside. The shouts of my inner critic began to quieten down. I realised that they would never stop completely, but the fact that they were not dominating my mind was an incredible breakthrough. There was something else, however. Something that was softer and quieter was dancing at the edges of my consciousness. Another voice was whispering to me; a voice that I have come to know very well indeed. This was the voice of my heart.

As I stared into my eyes, what I eventually saw looking back was me. I realise that may sound as though I'm stating the obvious, but I mean the real me. The one that is stripped of all criticisms, judgements and loathing. The one that isn't dependent on body size, any level of outward success, or compares herself to everyone on social media. This me was my soul; the true essence of who I am. The part of me that is whole, complete and eternal. It is the light within, and it was the brightest light I had ever seen!

As I softly gazed at my reflection, I heard my heart whisper, *'You are not this body. You are love. Love yourself.'* Tears of pure happiness sprang to my eyes as the words hit me; the power within them greater than anything in the known Universe. I knew in that instant that was true. For it didn't matter how much I judged or criticised myself on the outside, within I am love and nothing can ever change that. I smiled at my reflection and knew then that my journey on the path of really loving myself had begun.

I am not special or unique in this tale either. We all have this love and light within us, no matter how much you deny it or struggle to see it. Like me, you may find it hard to accept the concepts of self-love straight away. Even if you understand the ideas logically, you are dealing with years of built-up beliefs and experiences that started in your childhood, and your mind is not going to reject these straight away. We can cling on to the status quo, even when we know it isn't the best option for us.

The first step is the most important one, and it is simply to acknowledge that you deserve to be happy. This may sound like a *'duh, well obviously!'* comment, but you'd be surprised how many people struggle with this. Some have such low self-esteem that the thought of living a life of fulfilment, abundance, and joy can seem like wishful thinking; certainly nothing that they're ever going to have for themselves. Even if they wish their life could be better, they will sabotage themselves at the starting line because they don't fully believe it can be theirs, or that they deserve it. And yet, if you can accept the fact that you deserve to be happy, then you can start to come to terms with the idea that maybe you're not as awful as you believed yourself to be, and perhaps you do deserve love after all.

One baby step at a time though. Let's say for argument's sake that you see yourself as someone that is never really going to have a happy life. Things have been beyond difficult so far, and you don't see how they could ever improve. These concepts of happiness and loving yourself may be perfectly fine for people who aren't struggling, but some don't live in a fantasy world, right? And, let's say by some miracle that you did have all your dreams come true, who's to say that it would last? After all, you've ballsed up before, so why shouldn't you do so in the future?

Stop.

Breathe.

Go and sit in front of a mirror, preferably one that shows all of your face without you having to move it. Remove all distractions for ten minutes.

(Pause here until you have time to do this exercise if you can't do it right now. Don't skip this step believing it to be not that important; it really is!)

No phones, TV, or other people for ten whole minutes. Just

you and the mirror. Now, look at yourself. I mean, *really* look. Look into your own eyes and hold that gaze. Feel free to blink but do your best not to look away.

I know this is going to feel uncomfortable for you. You may squirm with embarrassment, giggle nervously, or even find it hard to look at your reflection at all for longer than a couple of seconds. No matter what your reaction, it's important that you stay with the exercise. The point is to see past all the judgements, the stresses, and the pressures that are piled upon you. Look past the surface of what your outer body looks like and see what lies behind. I promise you, the more you look into your own eyes, the more you will see the real you. The you that is eternal; the you that is love. As you look into your reflected eyes, wrap your arms around yourself and say, *'I love you.'* It doesn't matter whether you fully believe it or not in that minute; in fact, it's more important to do this if you **don't** believe in what you're saying. It's easy to go to war on your fear and fight the negativity, but what it actually needs is love. Love the criticisms, the negativity and the fear: all of it. The only way you're going to make real and long-lasting shifts in your life is to pour love on to all of it.

Engaging with this exercise shifts your mindset and helps you start to comprehend the possibility that you deserve your love too. And that first step cannot be underestimated. Until you understand this, you will end up in a never-ending battle with your own negative ego; one that is exhausting, demoralising, and downright boring!

I hope you found it to be a truly transformative experience. It can almost be surprising to realise that this light has been within you this whole time, but you've never taken the time to look. Don't feel guilty about that – most people don't take the time to truly look within themselves. Some are afraid of what they might find if they do: either something bad or, even worse, nothing at all. But, like I said to you before, we **all** have this light within us, no matter who we are.

Now that you've engaged with one practical exercise on this journey of self-love, I'm going to introduce you to some more. I solemnly swear to hold your hand every step of the way. I know right now you may feel like a newly-born foal, gently taking your first steps and trying not to fall over. The further along on this journey you go, the more confidence you will gain in yourself and the process.

Let's take the next step then, shall we? One that may seem even more knee shaking than looking at your own reflection. But, if we're going to move forwards, it's important to understand where we have been.

# Making Peace with Your Past

My parents got divorced when I was eight years old, and I moved with my mum from the north of England to the Midlands; two and a half hours away. My dad did his best to come and see me – he'd make the trip down to me once a month, and I'd go back up north in the school holidays. And yet, I have carried a lot of upset and hurt over this relationship for many years.

Why is this?

We all put our parents on a pedestal. They are like Gods to their children. They have all the answers, and love and protect us unconditionally. For me, I had an idealised view of what my parents should be. Years of TV shows, films, and stories that painted parents in a certain way. When they don't quite live up to that unreachable standard (who can?), you somehow see them as failing in some way. Sad, but true.

As children, all of us grow up idolising our fathers.

They are our ultimate heroes. The ones who have the answers. The ones who always guide us. No matter what they do, they are perfect and stand by us, no matter what the circumstances. While fathers might say they love their children equally, we all know that there is nothing as special as a father-daughter relationship. For a girl, her father is her absolute favourite man in the world. And every other man she meets has to match up to the standards set by her father.

And yet, the relationship I have had with my dad felt as though it didn't quite match up to this idealised dream. I'd watch films like *Meet Joe Black* and *What Women Want* and literally sob my eyes out at the tender moments between the father and daughter. I'd dream about my dad and I sharing one of those moments ourselves, but we never did. I know now that my dad had not had a close emotional relationship with his own parents; after all, we parent how we have been parented ourselves. He wasn't abusive in any way, he just wasn't as emotionally open or available as I wanted him to be. I felt as though he didn't give me the attention and support that I needed, despite the fact that I tried to talk to him a few times over the years.

For many years, I have blamed my low self-esteem in part on my dad, and this is unfair. Parents are not infallible superheroes that never put a foot wrong. They are human beings and will do their best; just like the rest of us. It's time to take our parents off their pedestals and see them for who they really are: flawed human beings who are trying their best to get things right.

Once I got my head around that, I saw that putting all the blame at my dad's door was wrong, and also meant I was diverting responsibility away from myself. Yes, we have all been through awful experiences as we've moved through life; that's just the nature of things. But, that doesn't mean we should use them as our get out of jail free card forever. At some point, we have to stop being a victim of the past and make our peace with it. We have to let it go.

When you carry around the weight of the past on your shoulders, you really are making life very difficult for yourself, and unnecessarily too. Baggage like this stops you living the happy life that you deserve. It weighs you down, becomes unbearably painful, and stops you from moving forward. If you truly want to love yourself, it's time to forgive.

We all have baggage from our past, some worse than others. It's rare to go through life without experiencing pain to some degree. And it can be awfully tempting to carry it around with us. After all, surely, we're justified in still being hurt and angry! Someone else has hurt us! If we forgive them, aren't we basically saying that what they did to us was okay?

No.

If someone has hurt you, that is never okay. I'm not here to condone that, or excuse anything. Bad behaviour towards you is never okay.

But...

When you carry around the pain and anger throughout your life, all that happens is that it hurts **you**. The other person involved rarely cares that you're still feeling so much pain, but it can really have a negative impact on your life. In the vast majority of cases, your anger and hurt won't even be registered by the other person, let alone have any effect on them. It is like drinking poison every day and expecting the other person to die.

In truth, carrying around all of this pain, hurt, and anger long after the event does nothing but poison you. And, you're still giving that other person all of your power. They are still having a profound effect upon your life, even if they have long moved on with their own life. If you are truly going to start to love yourself, then you have to take back your own power. To realise that this kind of past-baggage carrying is keeping you firmly stuck, in both the past and your own misery.

*A loving person lives in a loving world. A hostile person lives in a hostile world. Everyone you meet is your mirror.*
*– Ken Keyes*

I truly realised that with my ex-husband. Even after he had moved out, I was still carrying around so much anger and hurt towards both him and what had happened between us. I felt the need to continually talk it through, especially with my family. And, of course, I justified this by saying it was helping me process everything I had been through. In truth, however, it was doing little but causing me more pain and holding me back. It was the equivalent of picking at a scab over and over again so it could never fully heal; especially as I continued to talk about him with such bile.

I realised that consistently going over the past was keeping me stuck in that energy. It wouldn't have been so damning if I was in a space of total love for myself, but I found my outpourings contained a lot of anger and guilt towards myself. All relationships take two people to make it work, and two people to make it not work. I was giving myself a hard time for the part I had played in that relationship with my ex-husband. I blamed myself for entering into a relationship that I wasn't 100% sure of; for rushing things along without taking the time to stop and consider if it was what I really wanted; and for staying in the relationship longer than I should've done. My ex was no angel, but I was holding a lot of blame and guilt towards myself too, and I knew that this energy was not serving me in any way.

In actual fact, holding all the stress and guilt within was affecting my health. Having suffered with severe cramps and bloating within my stomach for months, I was finally diagnosed with stress-related Irritable Bowel Syndrome (IBS). That really was the turning point for me. It was one thing to wonder whether holding these negative emotions was proving to be a block mentally and emotionally. You can almost dismiss those thoughts and keep trying to power through it all. But, I couldn't ignore this. My body was literally screaming at me that I needed to make changes. I was clueless about how to fully release everything though. Thankfully, as I have seen time and time again, when the student is ready the teacher will appear.

Since 2010, I have worked as a psychic, giving people guidance through using oracle cards and my own abilities. Like many psychics, though, I struggle to give the kind of reading to myself that I give to others. I am too subjective and emotionally tied to my situation, so I find it hard to be objective enough. I've even been known to reshuffle a deck of oracle cards and pull another card if I don't like the one I've drawn! As such, I look to others to give me the guidance I seek, and one of them is my friend Jolene Trister.

Jolene is a wonderfully gifted human being. Her creativity and compassion are truly unprecedented. Not only is she an amazing psychic herself, but she also founded *Real Raw Being* magazine, which is a publication that seeks to offer enlightenment to all who read it. I knew unequivocally that Jolene would be able to help me.

I wasn't wrong! From the beginning, Jolene could clearly see how the guilt and anger over my ex-husband was affecting me and holding me back. She provided concise information of what I already knew, but her guidance went further than that. Rather than simply telling me the issues and allowing me to deal with them myself, Jolene gave me a ritual to do that proved to be life changing. I want to share this with you now, so that you too can release any pain, anger, guilt or shame that may be having a negative effect on you.

I set around two or three hours to myself. No children, no phones, nothing. I knew it was important to fully immerse myself in the work, and it would be damn near impossible if I was being distracted every few minutes.

First of all, I sat and wrote a letter to my ex. This was not going to be something that he, or anyone else, was ever going to see. It wasn't a letter to pop in the post or cause any more drama. The point was to use the page as my sounding board; to get **everything** out that was clogging up my brain about my ex or our whole time together. The key was to let the words come, without editing or censoring. It didn't matter what I was writing, how it sounded, what my handwriting looked like, or even if I had good spelling or punctuation! What mattered was that I wrote every single emotion that was connected to that whole experience out of my head and down on to the paper.

I wrote that letter for nearly an hour, my pen flying across the page. Once I had finished, I picked up all the pieces of paper and read them aloud. I was shocked to see how much venom and anger those pages contained. I knew the experience had clearly affected me; how could such a stressful situation not? But, to clearly see the uncensored truth of my feelings was something that even surprised me. The letter was raw; I felt as though I had been cut open.

Now came the next step of the ritual: to release the energy fully. It wasn't enough to simply write everything down, nor to read it out loud. To fully release myself from such profoundly negative energy, I needed to release all of that energy up to the Universe. So, making sure that I did it as safely as possible, I burnt the letter outside (I got some very strange looks from the neighbours, I can tell you!). As I watched the paper burn and smoke rise up into the sky, I felt a literal weight lift off my chest. A weight that had been there for so long that I had barely noticed it. Once the pot was filled with ashes, I tipped them into the soil; to transform the negative energy into something positive.

Once this part of the ritual was complete, it was important to undertake the next part. I ran myself a salt bath to cleanse away any residual negativity from my body so that I could move forward with a clean slate. Whilst in the bath, I played meditation music and allowed myself to visualise the biggest and happiest future I did want for myself.

Finally, I wrote another letter. Rather than being an outpouring of pain, this letter was to the Universe where I affirmed what I wanted for my life. I wrote each statement in the present tense with the words 'I am' at the start. No two words are more powerful that I am, for you are affirming whatever follows them as your truth. Writing each statement as though it was already mine meant that I was affirming this as my truth. If I had written, 'I would like,' all that would have happened would be that I would've delayed them manifesting in my life. I read this letter aloud too once I had finished it, but I didn't burn this one. To this day it is still pinned up to the door of my wardrobe. It is something I see all of the time and, every time I do, I reaffirm my intentions for my life.

So, did this ritual help me?

In a word, absolutely!

Since completing it, I have found that the way I feel towards my ex-husband is not as venomous or raw. I still have to see him regularly, as my twins go to stay with him every other week, and it's important for them that their parents are at least able to be civil to one another. More than this, however, my IBS has all but literally disappeared! It's amazing how such a seemingly simple ritual can have such a profound effect on releasing the pain from the past, and I urge you to give it a try too. It could prove to be just the thing to turn your life around for the better!

Making peace with your past is an essential step in learning to love yourself. The effects of not doing this can be far reaching and incredibly damaging in every area of your life. It could potentially stop you having the happiness you deserve to have, especially as you could end up with a real sense of self-blame, guilt, shame, and anger if you don't. These things are not going to make the path to self-love any easier!

Please remember that you did the best you could at the time. Your past has helped to shape you into the person you are, but it doesn't need to define you. You are not the person you used to be, and it's incredibly likely that you would do things differently if you had the chance to live your past events again. Your past is a part of you, but it's not all that you are. You can't change it, no matter how much you want to, but it's important to try and make peace with it. You deserve to be living a life that is centred around giving yourself the love, respect and compassion you deserve, and letting go of the negativity that's attached to the past will be a key step in doing just that.

# Protect Yourself

As I opened up my heart to myself, it quickly became apparent that there are people in life who are not on the same journey. When you're a good person and you try to see the best in others, you like to think that everybody else is the same as you, but sadly that's not the case. In life you will meet people who are intentionally malicious, and many who do not realise just how devastating an impact they can potentially have on your life through their own actions and words. Case in point, there was a woman on the fringes of my life that tried to do just that. For the sake of privacy, let's call her Emma.

I'd known Emma for just over a year. My twins and her daughter were in the same class at school. Like many mums in the playground, we ended up chatting and she seemed perfectly pleasant. She was always friendly, sympathetic, and someone who would listen to your problems. When I first met Emma, my ex-husband was still living with me, even though I'd long since told him that I didn't love him anymore. Life was incredibly stressful, and it was wonderful knowing I had a friend who I could offload to and talk with about my problems.

But, as you know, my situation eventually **did** change. My ex-husband moved out, and I was free from living under that constant pressure. I felt like a caged bird who had suddenly been set free. I believed that Emma would be happy for me. After all, she was my friend and she knew just how awful things had been for me because I'd told her everything that had gone on. And initially, she was. But, I soon noticed a subtle shift that became harder and harder to ignore.

You see, when some people's lives aren't that great and they're not terribly happy, they tend to surround themselves with others who are also struggling. Misery loves company, and it can become quite comforting to know that there are others going through similar or even worse things as you. When one of these friends turns their life around for the better, rather than being happy for them, they can become jealous, bitter and resentful. Your joy highlights the contrast with their own unhappiness, and they find it hard to get away from that.

And that's what happened with Emma. As the weeks rolled by, I noticed that she started to become more distant with me and regularly went and spoke to other mums; most of the time barely saying two words to me. Old habits die hard, and her actions reared up all my old patterns of thinking that I had been trying so hard to turn around. In my eyes, her distancing herself from me was my fault. I could hear the negative thoughts roaring up louder than ever:

*'You don't deserve friends.'*
*'No one likes you.'*
*'You're so horrible.'*

All of my self-hatred had loomed up like a threatening thunder cloud, and I seemingly forgot all of the positives I had been working towards. In that moment, I couldn't see that her behaviour was a symptom of her own issues (hindsight is a wonderful thing). All I could see was that it had to be my fault in some way. I didn't even have the courage to go and ask her about how she was treating me; even my fears of confrontation had reared up. I was terrified of what she could potentially say, especially that she might confirm all of my dark thoughts. So, instead I tried to smile it out... on the outside at least. I believed that burying my head in the proverbial sand was the best solution to the problem.

Thank goodness for my mum! I swear, no one knows me better than she does, and she could see through the fake smiles in a heartbeat. Talking through the situation with her allowed me to gain the perspective that I'd been seriously lacking. My mum helped me to consider the possibility that Emma's actions were not a reflection of me but were symbolic of her own deep-seated issues. As soon as I switched on that lightbulb of comprehension, I saw how truly ridiculous my negative thoughts had been. The situation with Emma was one that still upset me, but I could see that allowing it to destroy my attempts at loving and accepting who I am was a really unhealthy thing for me to do. I began to reaffirm all of the positive work I had been doing towards changing my thoughts from self-hate to self-love and got back on track. The dark clouds parted and the sun came out once again.

And that's what you need to be **so** aware of on this journey to loving yourself! Believe me, you may want to think that everyone you know has the same morals and values as you do, but sadly this just isn't the case. You will come across two kinds of people on your journey:

1. Those who have many deep-seated issues that they're not dealing with; either because they're not even aware of them, or because they're choosing to ignore them altogether. Rather than looking to make their own lives better, they project their insecurities out on to you.
2. Those who are consciously malicious and manipulative for their own selfish needs, and who don't care whom they hurt to get what they want.

I'm not here to freak you out. The majority of those people who will upset you in some way will fall into the first category. Although category two people do exist in the world, there aren't as many of them as the media and Hollywood scriptwriters would have you believe. I don't want you to go out into the world with fear in your heart and deep suspicion of everyone you meet!

It's important to understand, however, that you are going to meet people who aren't always going to treat you with the kindness and respect you deserve, either consciously or unconsciously. It's just the way that life is. The point isn't to try and remove them altogether, but to equip yourself so that you're able to protect yourself better. Removing people like this from the world is unrealistic. At certain points in our lives we all lash out at others because of our own pains and insecurities. We can be the nicest person in the world and still have a bad day that leaves its negative impact on others. If we looked to get rid of people who hurt others, the world would be a very empty space.

But, just because you can't control the kind of people who surround you all of the time, doesn't mean they necessarily have to have the same impact upon your life. When you're in the space of not loving yourself, it's easy to see how people like this can have such a negative effect on you. After all, your opinion of yourself is already on the floor, and all the other person's words or actions are doing is confirming that for you. In your mind, their nastiness is simply proof that your low opinion of yourself is justified. But, loving yourself is no guaranteed protection against these people; you have to consciously put boundaries in place every day to keep yourself safe. I will explain what these boundaries are in a minute, but I want to tell you a story first that demonstrates just how dangerous these negative people can be if you're not trying to protect yourself from them.

When I was 15, I dated the brother of my best friend for a few months. Although I can see now that it wasn't love, it certainly felt that way at the time. He was a couple of years older than me, and I thought he was just amazing. All tattoos, smoking and doing whatever he wanted. He oozed cool to my 15-year-old self, and when he asked me out, I felt like all my birthdays and Christmases had come at once. I was like a dopey-eyed puppy, following him round and hanging on his every word. I guess, for him, it was an ego boost at first to have a girl so besotted with him, but that behaviour can become beyond annoying after a while. Even the most arrogant and narcissistic man wants more from a relationship than a limpet. Not surprisingly, he dumped me after about three months and went back to his ex-girlfriend.

Did I chalk it up to experience and move on?

What do you think?

Yes, I bawled like a newborn baby when he finished things with me; my broken heart smashing into a million pieces. In this devastated state, I decided to do the one thing that made sense to me in that moment: I'd make him jealous. I figured if he saw me draped over someone else, he was bound to come running back to me and everything would be great again. I also realised that my ex needed to actually see me with someone new to get jealous, so I decided to date his friend.

Yes, I know, not a smart move on my part, but you don't tend to make the smartest moves when you're 15, do you?

Now, I need to paint you a picture of my targeted man. This is important because you'll quickly realise how warped my mind was in this moment, as well as clearly demonstrating how low my own sense of self-worth truly was. My ex's friend was older... six years older than me to be precise. Yes, I was a 15-year-old about to date a 21-year-old. Now I have children of my own I can see how bonkers that sounds, and slightly creepy on his part. But the age difference wasn't the only issue. This was a man who was very overweight and smelt constantly of bad body odour. Mm... what a catch! On the plus side, he had his own car and, as I said, he was friends with my ex. The plus points were what I focused on and I put my fingers in my ears to everything else. Surely if it meant getting my ex back it was worth putting up with a few weeks of inconvenience?

This man didn't know about my plan, of course. He was someone who hadn't had much luck on the dating scene, so he seemed to be overjoyed when I asked him out. Before long, we were zipping round town in his car – us in the front and my ex with his new girlfriend in the back. Christ! Even writing that makes me want to time travel back and smack myself around the face! It's beyond crazy that I allowed myself to go through a situation like that; even more when you consider that it was me who created it.

Hands up if you thought my plan worked?

I'm guessing we all know that it fell flatter than a pancake.

My ex was too wrapped up in his new girlfriend to give two hoots what I did, and I was becoming more frustrated and thoroughly fed up. I wasn't back in the arms of the man who I'd convinced myself that I loved and, worse still, I had some overweight, smelly man to contend with. Finally, thankfully, I came to my senses. I realised that it would be best for me to walk away from the situation I'd created, for it was doing nothing but upsetting me.

What I hadn't factored into my plan, however, was how my 'boyfriend' would take it. I was so caught up in my own emotions and drama that I didn't even consider the possibility that he may be upset by me ending things with him. I wish now that I'd been a bit more aware and protected myself more than I had.

I invited him round to tell him that I didn't want to see him anymore. Up until this point, I had only kissed him. I was a 15-year-old girl who was only dating this man to make her ex jealous of course. Kissing him was bad enough, and the thought of even considering anything else made my stomach turn over. I hadn't considered the fact that this man was 21 with all that age entails. And, on hindsight, I can see now what he must have been thinking: my girlfriend has invited me over to her empty house, maybe she's ready to take things to the next level.

I sat him down and told him that I didn't think things were working out between us and I didn't want to see him anymore. I expected him to cry maybe, or to storm off in a rage. What I didn't expect was him to launch himself at me and try to kiss me. I was alarmed as the weight of this man came on top of me, and wild panicked thoughts raced through my head. What was he going to do? Was he going to try and sexually assault me?

It was probably only a few seconds before the phone rang, but it felt like hours. Desperately, I said, *'That'll be my parents calling to tell me they're on their way home.'* Those words were enough to stop him in his tracks, and he frantically pulled himself to his feet before practically running out my front door. I never saw or heard from him again, and it wasn't too long afterwards that I met the boy that was to be my first proper serious boyfriend. The memories from that time linger at the edges of my mind like a ghost, the realisation of what might have been the outcome still making my heart beat a little faster to this day.

I never told my parents what had happened that afternoon, neither did I tell anyone else about it. In my head, I blamed myself for what had occurred. I had dated him when I knew I shouldn't. I was only 15 and he was a grown man of 21. I had invited him round when I knew I was going to be home alone. I genuinely believed that people would be disgusted and angry with me if I was honest about what happened, so I ignored it and carried on with my life.

How does all this tie in with the concept of loving yourself? When that situation happened to me all those years ago, the idea of loving myself was completely alien to me. Consequently, I didn't respect or value myself at all. I believe that played a big part in me not telling anyone about it. On some level, my opinions of myself meant I almost believed that I deserved what had happened. Yes, that's how low my self-esteem was. It wasn't so much a case that I had done anything to deserve what he had done, for there is never any justification for abusing your power in that way. But, I genuinely believed that it was symptomatic of my own sense of worth.

Reading this now makes me feel sick, but I can't deny how messed up my head was at that point. If anything happened to me like that now, I would tell someone else about it in a heartbeat, no question. The thing is, I know my low sense of worth is not a rare or strange occurrence. In truth, I know there are millions of people out there who also have an incredibly low opinion of themselves, and who consequently put up with things they really shouldn't. How many stay in abusive relationships? How many people are making excuses for being treated badly by others, or even blame themselves for getting hurt? In their low opinion they truly believe that they deserve it on some level. But, having this false belief can bring you untold trauma that no one deserves to be subjected to. It's **never** okay for anyone to hurt you. There are **no** excuses, justifications, or reasons why; **never ever!**

It may be tempting to think that these things don't apply to you. After all, you are heading off on the path to self-love with higher self-esteem; surely that protects you from situations like this? How I wish it were that simple. How I wish I could promise you that this love-filled path would make you immune from others' crappy behaviour.

Sadly, no. No matter where you are on the road of self-love, you will always come across people who are controlling, manipulative and abusive. As I said before, not everyone is as loving and kind as you are, no matter how much you may wish them to be so. What loving yourself does give you is the power to deal with these people in a better way.

When you start to bring more love into your life for yourself, you will naturally start to shine brighter. And you may even shine brighter than people around you; and that can kick up some potential issues for you. In an ideal world, everyone would be so pleased for you that you are so clearly happier than you have ever been. Those who truly love you want you to be happy, and they will celebrate your new sense of self-worth and self-love with you. But, sadly, not everyone around you is going to be in the same celebratory mood. But, these people will prove to be your biggest teachers on this path.

*It's not your job to like me... it's MINE!*
*– Byron Katie*

Those who are not supportive of this new path for you may feel that way for a number of reasons. They may not be happy within their own lives and loved having a 'misery buddy' to share their drama with. Now you are on the rise, they may feel you are leaving them behind. Or, perhaps you are inadvertently highlighting how they feel about themselves and that makes them feel super uncomfortable. Or, maybe it's a simple case of jealously where they don't like seeing anyone apparently doing better than themselves. Whatever the reason, it can lead to all kinds of nasty behaviour on their part: gossiping; turning their back on you; bullying; and other things that have the potential to derail you off your path.

Consider this though, when there is someone in your life who is treating you this way, it can actually prove to be the biggest lesson for you. Everything happens for a reason, and each situation (no matter how good or bad) comes along to help us grow and evolve. What can these lessons be?

Assertiveness is a big one. Being assertive is something that many people struggle with, and yet it is actually one of the most important things to bring into your life. I think many people worry that they'll be viewed as being aggressive, or they imagine all kinds of awful consequences as a result of trying to deal with other people's bad behaviour in an assertive way.

Assertiveness can be taken to this extreme, of course, but the two things don't naturally go hand in hand. Being assertive actually means being self-assured and confident. In truth, it's all about balance. It requires being honest about your wants and needs, whilst still considering the rights, needs and wants of others. Your self-assuredness gives you the strength to get your points across in a way that is firm, fair and with empathy.

In terms of people not supporting you and actually trying

to sabotage your efforts to be happier within and without, being assertive means learning how to communicate what you need in any given moment. It means identifying that the other person's behaviour is detrimental to your well-being and requesting calmly but firmly that it needs to stop. It's not screaming, swearing, and throwing your toys out of the pram to get your own way. It means that you don't allow yourself to become a victim, and you refuse to tolerate any kind of situation that isn't for your highest good. If you have communicated to someone that they are not treating you as you deserve, and they refuse to stop, then you need to remove them from your life. Assertiveness is not lip service or half-arsed measures. It's doing what's right for you. It's self-respect, self-love and real self-care.

Whilst this may sound logical and a positive thing on paper, in practice it can be something different entirely. The thought of having to be assertive can be really intimidating in itself, especially when you haven't done it before. However, if you have a plan in place of how you can be more assertive in your daily life, it will help to ease some of those concerns. After all, most fears stem from feeling out of control. Putting in proactive steps is just the ticket to help you regain a greater sense of control.

First of all, it's really important that you voice your wants and needs. You can't wait for someone else to recognise what's going on inside your head. You could be waiting forever! For all of your hope that people are mind readers, the vast majority of people won't know what you're feeling or thinking unless you tell them. And making the assumption that they do is only going to lead to more trouble and stress in the long run for everyone. This doesn't need to be done in a finger-pointing, accusatory way, but in a manner that is both constructive and sensitive. Stick to the facts of the situation and try to use 'I' statements: *'I want'*, *'I need'*, and *'I feel'*. Doing so will mean that the other person is more likely to hear what you're saying and to respond in a more positive way. If you communicate with lots of 'you' statements in contrast, the other person may feel attacked and will be more likely to respond defensively and aggressively back to you.

Always try to let empathy lead the way. Even the most obnoxious and difficult person still wants to be understood, and your assertiveness will be more likely to have a positive outcome if the person you're talking to feels you understand how they're feeling. You can't control anyone but yourself of course, and you can never fully plan exactly what another person will do or say. But, having tools in place for you to approach a problem in an assertive manner means you're staying aligned with your own integrity and self-respect.

I wish I had realised these things before my encounters with those who hurt me emotionally, mentally and physically, but it's clear that my life up until this point has been a learning process. Would I have wished to have gone through certain things? Absolutely not. Does understanding that everything happens for a reason excuse the behaviour of those who wronged me? Hell, no. No matter what someone has been through in their lives, or how you can see in hindsight that the situation they've put you through has made you a stronger person, that does not justify their behaviour. Nothing could do that, ever.

What I do know is that I'm more aware, assertive, and stronger now than I have ever been. This energy doesn't necessarily protect me from getting hurt again in the future, but it does mean that my reaction will be completely different from how I reacted to situations in the past. I know I deserve better, so much better in every sense. I deserve respect, compassion and fairness. And, because I know that, I will ensure that my own assertiveness leads the way. I will not ignore bad behaviour towards myself from anyone. Truly, if you want love and respect, you have to give it to yourself first. Set the bar for your life, and let your self-love be at the forefront of all your encounters.

# Let Go

I think my ego likes to hold on to fear tighter than a toddler with their blankie. One of the biggest challenges I have encountered on this self-love journey so far is not failing to make peace with those around me, but actually making peace within myself. For the majority of our lives, we look to those around us to teach us things, and fix things for us when life doesn't go as planned. Whether it's your teachers, parents, or anyone else who has been the person you've looked to do these things for you, the issue comes when you realise that the self-love path is one that you need to walk alone. That's not to say that others can't support you on the journey, but they can't actually do it for you; even if they really want to, and you want to let them!

What is the reason for this?

Well, each person's life is unique and subjective. We all have our own issues, beliefs, experiences and insecurities to deal with. Each one of us is as individual and unique as a fingerprint or a snowflake. So, what may have worked for one person isn't necessarily going to work for you; and that's okay! Even the most experienced and knowledgeable people in the world don't know everything, and your own blocks and issues are unique to you. This book is a guide to what I've been through and what's worked for me, but that doesn't mean that every word is going to resonate with you. You find your own way through. The key is to realise that you want to live a happier and more fulfilled life, and that loving yourself is an important step to helping you achieve that. Once you have committed to making that your reality, then how you get there is secondary. Nothing is as important as your own happiness.

As well as learning to make peace with my past and protect myself, there have been a number of things that I have had to consciously work at to let go. Things that were not only pulling me down into self-hate rather than lifting me into self-love, but were also robbing me of the chance to find real happiness to boot. One of those issues has been the fear that I won't be accepted for who I am.

*Your problem is you're... too busy holding onto your unworthiness.*
*– Ram Dass*

At first, I thought this fear came from the bullying at school, but I was given the opportunity to understand that my issues stem much further back than I could have ever fully realised. I have become a big fan of meditation over the last few years. Learning to meditate has allowed me not only to open spiritually, but has also been a massive benefit for my mental and emotional health. Having the space to unplug from the stresses and pressures of modern life, as well as allowing me to fully process the concerns I'm dealing with, has seen me feeling more in control of my inner self than ever. Normally, I focus on my breathing and the quietness inside of me, but there have been many times when I have consciously chosen to listen to a pre-recorded guided meditation. These are widely available on YouTube and have allowed me to work on such things as clearing my chakras, relaxing, and mindfulness. There was one I did in particular, however, that helped me understand myself in a way that had been unavailable to me before.

Working with Darren Linton on his Guided by Angels course (http://www.guidedbyangels.info/guidedbyangels.shtml), I went through a meditation that unlocked the doors to one of my past lives. All the work I had done with Darren previously had been gentle, loving and uplifting, but it was clear that the Universe had a bigger plan for me:

*During that meditation, I walked along a long corridor with doors either side. I had the deep knowing that each door was representative of a past life I had experienced, but I also knew that it was the door at the end of the corridor that was the most important for me to witness at that time. As I entered, it was strange in the fact that I was watching it play out in front of me like a movie, and yet I was also in the body of my former self at the same time; I had first and third person perspective.*

*I was a woman of around the age of 30, and I was living in a cottage on my own on the edge of a large forest. I had no concept of where the lifetime was based, but the lush forest reminded me of many European landscapes I have seen. Not far from my cottage was a village, and the villagers were regularly coming down to visit me, each one leaving me with a bottle or small brown parcel in their hands. On entering the cottage, I saw that my home was filled with endless jars, baskets and bottles of herbs, plants, and other natural artefacts. In the middle of my home was a cauldron over a fire, and I deduced that I was the medicine woman and healer for the people of that village. My work brought me untold joy, and I loved being able to help people with all manner of problems. Life was peaceful, happy and fulfilling.*

*I was then taken to another time, some years after the original scene. Villagers were huddled together in hushed whispers, their furtive glances shooting suspicion and fear in my direction. Within the village was the icon of a large cross, and it became apparent that a religious fervour had taken over the people, with an attached sense of doubt and anxiety placed upon my work in the progress. No longer was I seen as the healer, but accusations were soon flying that I was in league with Lucifer himself.*

*In the dead of night, as I lay sleeping, several villagers burst into my cottage and dragged me from my bed; hands clamped firmly over my mouth so my screams were muffled in the darkness. As I thrashed and kicked, they carried me deep into the forest, my heart sinking at the realisation of what was about to occur. Finally, after what seemed like hours of walking, they stopped and thrust me roughly against a large tree. Ropes were wound tightly around me, and my arms and legs bound to the rough bark. Then, without so much as a word uttered, they turned and left me, my fate sealed in one action.*

*For days I stood, bound to that old tree. At the start, I called out, my desperate cries pleading for someone to help me. My severe thirst and hunger pains made my head swim, but I was spared the torture of starving to death. Instead, the birds came. Beaks, claws and feather ravaged me, but my fight had gone. By the time anyone walked that path again, my soul had long since left my broken body.*

When my consciousness came back into my body, tears were streaming down my face. How awful to have gone through such a cruel and savage situation! Especially when all I had done was seek to help and heal the people of that village. Working with Darren and the angels, however, I knew I had to let the pain from that time go. If I was going to properly move on from that lifetime, I had to forgive all those involved and release it. It was clear that my fears of not being accepted for who I am had their roots in that time, for I was severely persecuted and suffered a terrible death just for being true to who I was. Subconsciously, the memories and fear still remained within my soul, and I knew it was time to allow myself to be fully free of them.

I called upon Archangel Michael to help me cut my cords. When you connect with another person, an etheric cord is formed between both of you. This cord of energy cannot be seen by your physical eyes, but we all have cords that attach us to others. When the relationship is loving and healthy, it can create a vibrant and energetic exchange between the people on either end. You both feel lit up from inside. But, when the relationship falls into fear, these cords mean you may feel drained, blocked and controlled; even when the other person is no longer part of your life. Unless the cord is disconnected, you will notice there are times in your life when you feel tired, flat or drained, but there is no knowable reason why you may feel this way. It's time for your cords of fear to be cut, and Archangel Michael is the perfect angel to help you do just that.

I mentally asked him to cut my cords of fear and attachment in all directions of space and time, and to send love and healing to all people involved. I then breathed deeply and allowed Archangel Michael to do this for me. I felt a sense of movement behind me and saw in my mind's eye that Michael was pulling the cords from me and cutting them with his sword of light; but none of it was painful in the slightest. When he had finished, it was as if a large weight had been removed from me; one that I hadn't even realised had been there. I felt lighter and there was a real sense that what had been weighing me down was now gone. Now, when I thought back to that past life, I was able to view the people's actions against me with compassion and forgiveness. Rather than seeing them as malicious and wicked, I saw that they had been brainwashed by the sudden onslaught of religion upon the village and were made to believe that my healing abilities were evil. In their eyes, their actions were justified and they were doing the work of God. It didn't mean that what they did was justified, but I knew that carrying around anger towards them was only hurting me. Finally, I was able to let it go.

The resulting effect upon my life was immediate. The fear of what other people would think about me and the worry that they wouldn't accept me for who I am vanished. I felt freer than I had ever done and could stand proud for the first time in my life and declare, 'This is who I am!' So many of us hide our lights because we hold an innate fear of being disliked or not accepted. But, when you do this, it becomes much harder to be able to give yourself the love you need and deserve. It's important to realise that you're not going to be liked and accepted by everyone you meet in life, and that's okay!

Let me ask you, do you like everyone you've ever met?

Have you even been able to accept someone else's differences every time you've come across them?

I know you want to say yes, but I also know the chances are you will have to say no to these questions. We all have our sets of beliefs, norms and values and, even with the best intentions in the world, there will be times when you find it hard to put into practice the notion of accepting people for who they are. And yet, we want to be liked and accepted by everyone we meet! Sadly, we can't have it both ways and, when we realise that not everyone is going to accept and like us, the freedom is immense! Suddenly, we can stop trying to be the beige and bland person we've been trying to be, and we can shine our light fully for who we actually are! Let me tell you something else too: when we come into full alignment with who we truly are, we will attract more people into our life who love us for being us! Wouldn't you rather have a close group of people who loved, supported and believed in you fully, rather than a large group who were more 'meh' about you? Quality over quantity every time.

The proof that I had truly shifted? Before the realisation of the effect of that past life, I had been terribly upset when I was labelled and gossiped about by people whom I used to see every day. When my eldest son was younger, he attended a local primary school near to where we lived. The other mums in the playground were nice enough to me at first, but things started to shift when they found out about my interests and work life. Discovering that I have a deep love of angels, crystals, spirituality and the paranormal placed a big wedge between us and I got called a witch. Now, I've nothing against witchcraft or Wicca in the slightest, but their labelling was done from a place of judgement, fear and trying to pull me down. In that instance, the name calling was truly upsetting, and took me emotionally back to my school days. Back then, I had started my fledgling journey into spiritual discovery, but soon stopped when the girls at school found out and bullied me for it. The distress of not being accepted for who I am was both real and painful, and I turned my light down so I wouldn't attract their unwanted attention.

After the past life work, all that changed! I actually wrote a long post on social media that proudly announced who I was and what I believed in, without feeling the need to apologise or justify any of it. Not only that, but I started to be more open to people in real life too. Before, I would say I was a psychic with embarrassment, as though the very idea of being connected with that work was something to be ashamed of. In the action of doing this, I actually made others view my work as something to be suspicious of, or to not take seriously. Once the shift had occurred within me, however, I could see the truth in all its glory. Since I have been working as a psychic, I have literally helped hundreds of people to find comfort, happiness, healing and peace. This is nothing to be ashamed or embarrassed about! In fact, I'm truly proud of the work I do, and I'll happily wave my flag from the rooftops now for all the world to see. I love who I am, and I'm bloody proud of it too.

Of course, letting go of this one aspect of fear wasn't enough. Like the glitziest mirror ball in the disco, my fear was multilayered and complex. Alongside the fear that I wouldn't be accepted for who I am, there was also the fear that I would be exposed for being a fake. That people would find me out for not being good enough, and I'd be called out for the imposter I believed myself to be.

Imposter Syndrome is a belief within that a person is totally inadequate and incompetent, despite evidence to the contrary. You feel as though you're always waiting to be found out, and when others do they'll laugh at you and reject you. Writer Valerie Young in her book, *The Secret Thoughts of Successful Women: Why Capable People Suffer from the Imposter Syndrome and How to Thrive in Spite of It,* has identified five subgroups of Imposter Syndrome:

1. The Perfectionist
2. The Superwoman/man
3. The Natural Genius
4. The Rugged Individualist
5. The Expert

Let's look at them one by one to explain the differences –

## The Perfectionist

When you're a perfectionist, you set goals for yourself that are unrealistic and excessive. Then, when you don't reach them, you experience doubts and anxiety that you're not good enough. You may also be a control freak, as you believe that if a job is going to be done properly, then it's best for you to do it yourself. Even when you are successful, you will believe it's not good enough and you could have done better.

**If you see yourself in this role, know that giving yourself praise and validation for the work you do is extremely important. It'll help to increase your esteem and boost you to try further ventures. Not only this, but you need to start projects before you're completely ready. If you wait for everything to be 'perfect' before you start, you could be waiting forever. Things are never 100% perfect, and you need to push yourself to try. You may surprise yourself (in a good way) if you do.**

## The Superwoman/man

You may be absolutely convinced that you're a phony amongst those you're surrounded with, and so will push yourself to work harder and longer to measure up to them. Working this way is a cover-up for your insecurities, and places you in a risky place for your health and relationships with others.

**If you recognise yourself in this role, know that you have to find a way to stop getting validation from others and discover a way to acquire it for yourself. If you only get it from others,**

it can really knock you if that is taken away. Look at your own skills and attributes. See your achievements to date, and know your own worth. In the same vein, it's important to learn to take constructive criticism without seeing it as a personal attack.

## The Natural Genius

You may judge yourself on your abilities rather than your efforts. In your eyes, if you have to work hard at something rather than being a natural at it, then you somehow see yourself as a failure. Just like the perfectionist, the natural genius sets the bar impossibly high for themselves. The difference is that the natural genius doesn't have harsh judgements of themselves from those expectations, but whether they can reach them on the first try. The moment something doesn't flow easily or quickly for them, then the fears set in.

**If you see this as you, please know that you're a work in progress, not a finished model. If you find things harder than you thought you would, see it as a sign for you to take a proactive step to make a change so you can find things easier next time.**

## The Rugged Individualist

You may feel as though you're not good enough because you've had to ask for help. Being a strong individual is one thing, but refusing help when you really need it in case you're seen as weak or not good enough is not helping you in any way.

**If this is you, start to switch things around by asking for help from others for the small, insignificant things. That way, you won't put so much weight behind them, and asking won't have a strong effect on your sense of worth. The more you can see that others can and want to help you, the more you can build up to the more important things.**

## The Expert

You may believe you have somehow tricked your employer into hiring you, and constantly worry that you'll be found out for being actually unknowledgeable and inexperienced for the role you have. The worst thing you can be called is an 'expert' because it makes those fears rise to the surface.

**If this flags up for you, know that there's no harm in asking for help. No one knows everything and we learn by reaching out to others. There's the notion of mentoring others. When you can teach and pass on your knowledge to others, it will help give you a better sense of being the capable person you really are.**

For me, I identify as The Expert out of all of them. All of the writing I have done, I have always worried that I wasn't good enough and it was just a matter of time until others knew it too. How do I keep trying to move past this fear? As the famous saying goes, I feel the fear and do it anyway! Yes, it's tough at times, especially when you receive any kind of rejection (as all writers do in their careers), but the passion for my dream is actually greater than the fear. I have found something that gives me an immense sense of passion and drive, and nothing can stop me doing it; not even my own fears and anxieties. Every time I do happen to receive a rejection, I make myself get back on the horse as quickly as possible so that the fears don't have much chance to grab hold and pull me down into inaction. Yes, it can be a powerful worry at times, but that doesn't mean it has to debilitate altogether. Loving yourself means putting your needs and dreams first, even when your hands are shaking with fear.

Please note that you are exactly where you need to be right now. Wherever you are in your own life, that is important for your own journey. Each situation is a pinpoint on the map of your life, and each stage gives you valuable lessons and experiences to draw from. If you do find yourself falling into a comparison trap, please know that doesn't mean that you're off-track or missing out. Everything will be alright in the end and, if it isn't alright, then it isn't the end. You are the writer, director, producer and star of your own life, and you get to decide what happens next.

Let go of anything that's blocking you from loving yourself and helping you to be happy. Remove the weights from around your mind and let yourself fly!

# Body Issues

*'You look beautiful!'*

Did I, really? How could they say that when there were so many reasons not to say it? I stared at the saleswoman and tried to muster up a smile.

*'Oh, thank you. I don't think I'll get it though. Maybe another day.'* That's what I said, but in my head, I was convinced that she was only telling me these things to get a sale out of me. Surely, she didn't mean it? I bet she actually thought that the top made me look like a beached whale, and a bloated one to boot. Smiling meekly, I shuffled back into the changing room and tried to pull the top up over my head... it wouldn't budge. Feeling the clammy sweat of panic starting to prickle over my skin, I tried to take the top down off my body, but still it wouldn't move. For ten painfully long minutes, I struggled to get that blasted top off me, but it may as well have been covered in glue before I put it on. Feeling my cheeks burning with a deep sense of shame, I poked my head back around the curtain.

*'Excuse me, could you come here please?'*

With eyes cast resolutely on the floor, I mumbled my predicament to this shop assistant and prepared to suffer the humiliation of having her yank the top over my head. Beautiful? I had never felt so blobby and ugly in my life. As soon as I was free, I grabbed my stuff and scuttled out of the shop as fast as my legs could carry me, a cloud of body issues hanging over me.

I have long had a love-hate relationship with my body, although it's mostly one that has been squarely focused on the hate end of the see-saw. Whenever I looked at myself in the mirror, all I could see were the parts of myself that I didn't like. For one, that I have an astigmatism in my right eye, for example, which means that it isn't as strong as my left. It's not too noticeable when I'm moving through my day, but each photograph of me may as well come with the gossip magazine's Hoop of Shame, for it's always the first thing I notice. Taking a selfie is more like taking 10–20 selfies and choosing the one that doesn't show my eye issue as much as the others.

This came to a head when I was a weekly contributor on the Facebook page of my friend, the writer Theresa Cheung. Each week, I would post an inspirational video or post, and I soon became known as the Angel Lady. I loved helping people, and my videos were getting thousands of views each week, all with really positive feedback. Then, one week, a lady (who I didn't know) made a six-word comment that floored me: *'I pray your eye gets fixed.'* Instantly, I was plunged down the hole of anxiety and body hating. My own issue that I had always been so careful to minimise had been spotted and drawn out for everyone to see. Although my friends and family reassured me, I was convinced that the whole world was now laughing at me and that no one would ever take me seriously again.

Melodramatic maybe?

In truth, that lady's comment was an important part of my self-love journey. She may not have realised it when she posted what she did, but her words were an important catalyst that allowed me to have a very honest dialogue with myself. If I was going to encourage others to love themselves and talk about how important self-love is for happiness, surely, I was doing everyone a disservice (including myself) by only allowing myself to love the parts of myself that I deemed suitable. The bits of me I didn't like were still the punching bags of my self-hatred and were proving to be real blocks that were preventing me from loving myself fully. If I was going to love myself, that had to be ALL of myself, and this woman's Facebook comment helped me to see that. Not that I was terribly happy about it, of course!

How did I flip things around? I went and sat back at the mirror. I knew it was time to look myself squarely in the eyes and see all the wonderful things they are able to do. Without them, I wouldn't be able to look into the faces of the people I love, indulge my favourite hobby of reading, or appreciate all the wonder and beauty that the world has to offer. Without my eyes, I would be stuck in the darkness of being blind, and I would've missed out on so much. Yes, my eye is weak, but it works! That in itself is a miracle, and I gave my eye and myself some much-needed love. Rather than focusing on what is wrong with the body part you're less than keen on, remember all the fantastic things that body part allows you to do! No matter what that body part is, if you didn't have it your life would be a lot harder than it is right now. That part of your body may not look the way you'd ideally like it to, but it is a fundamental part of who you are. Without some serious money and surgery, you can't change it, and it's healthier for your mental and emotional well-being to focus on loving it as it is, rather than hating it for what it's not.

Of course, sometimes there are things you can do to help yourself. Aside from my eye, the other main issue I've had with my body over the years is how much it's weighed. My weight has been up and down like a proverbial yo-yo, and there have been many times when I've not given my body the love, nurturing and care it deserves. Each time I have put the weight on, it's been the symptom of my emotional trauma at that time. Case in point was when I had given birth to my twins. For the four weeks prior to giving birth to them, I had been suffering with gastroenteritis. If you don't know what this is, it's an inflammation of the stomach and intestines that is caused by bacterial toxins or viral infection, and it leads to severe vomiting and diarrhoea (sorry if you're reading this whilst eating). Problem was, not only was I diagnosed with this after giving birth (the midwives and doctors weren't sure what was wrong with me for a long time), but it also triggered labour at 30 weeks. My twins were born weighing three and a half pounds each, and were put into the Special Care

Baby Unit for four weeks. Because the medical staff didn't know what was wrong with me, they kept me isolated after the birth too, in case I was infectious. Consequently, I wasn't able to see or hold either of my newborn babies for two days after they had been born. To say it was traumatic would be downplaying it completely.

I ended up also being diagnosed with post-natal depression a month or two after giving birth. Whether the events around the birth of my twins was a factor in my mental state is debatable, but I did end up being prescribed counselling and antidepressants. However, a side effect of my depression was mindless eating. When you're feeling in an emotionally negative place, you crave moments of pleasure and joy, and foods that are high in sugar and fat give you that instant gratification; until you've swallowed them that is. Then comes a tidal wave of guilt and shame that sends you plunging down even lower than you were before you ate whatever you had that wasn't good for you.

The result of all this? I ended up weighing 16st 8lb (105kg), which is 5 stone (31.7kg) heavier than I am now. Eating like this is the equivalent of self-harm, for I logically knew that my actions were bad for my physical, mental and emotional health, yet I couldn't stop the vicious cycle I had put myself in. Chocolate, cakes, biscuits, chips, pizza, curry – it all went into my body, and the effect was profound and devastating. From a UK size 12/14 to a size 20, I now hated my reflection in the mirror, and tried to avoid looking at myself as much as possible. But, it wasn't just my physical appearance that was affected; my health was being impacted too. As a teenager, I had suffered with mild asthma, however, this had all but disappeared into my twenties. Now, I was finding that my chest was tight all of the time, and even the gentlest of physical exertion was putting me majorly out of breath. My joints were starting to become exceedingly painful too, with my knees, back and hips noticeably very sore. Not great for a new mum who has to spend an awful lot of time on the floor and running up and down the stairs. Logically, I knew I had to stop the abuse I was putting myself through every day, but I felt lost and powerless as to how to actually do this.

At the time, my parents lived in the South-East of England, whilst I was still based in the Midlands. Although I spoke to my mum every day on the phone, I hadn't actually seen her in person for a while and had managed to hide the extent of my weight gain from her. My mum is a woman who has worked in the diet and fitness industry all her life, and I was deeply ashamed that her only child had put enough weight on to be classed as morbidly obese. When she came up to see me over Christmas, my weight was the literal elephant in the room. My mum initially didn't want to bring it up because she knew it would upset me, and I didn't want to talk about it because I was so embarrassed and disgusted by it all. As all good mums do though, she eventually took me to one side and talked to me about what was going on. Desperately, I tried to reassure her that I knew I had to do something about it and things would be okay, but at that point it was just words. I didn't fully believe what I was saying, and I was only saying them to placate her and stop her questioning. That all changed when she bought me a onesie.

My mum had bought me one for Christmas, and had to get me size 18, as this was the biggest size they stocked. As I put it on, I heard every stitch pull and stretch. They didn't tear completely, but I couldn't do up the buttons at the chest. Every person who is dealing with an addiction (and I genuinely believe I was addicted to food at this point) has a wake-up call that makes them realise without doubt that things need to change; they can't carry on the self-destructive path they're on. As I sat on my bed with the tears streaming down my face, I knew this was my moment. I knew then that I had to do something and quick. I was out of control and truly hated what I had done with my body. The next day, I Googled slimming clubs in my area, and I started dieting a week later.

Has my weight loss journey been a one-time thing? No. Like most people who have issues with their weight, I have had a few times when I've had to address what I'm doing and regain control, but that's okay. What's important is that I don't hate my body like I used to. Yes, when I put some weight back on it does affect my confidence and how I feel about myself, but I don't allow myself to spiral down like I used to. I refocus and regain control over what I'm doing. Because, ultimately, this is the most important thing to remember.

You only get one body for the duration of your life. Whether every inch of your body is how you would ideally like it to be or not, it's yours. Yes, you can diet, have cosmetic surgery, and use clever underwear and make-up to enhance what you have, but there are limits as to what you can do. At the end of the day, you can't have anyone else's body; you are stuck with the one you have. And, if you're going to go on this journey of loving yourself, then you have to find a way to love your body too; no matter what size, shape or form that may take.

If you focus primarily on what you look like, you're going to be on a slippery and rocky slope. The slightest off day or wobble will set you right back, so it's vital you switch your focus. Let your health be your main objective, not trying to desperately get some idealised perfect body that you see in magazines and billboards. (By the way, no one looks like that, not even the models themselves. Photoshop is key in every professional photograph now. Trying to look like the images you see is a one-way ticket to misery and self-hate.) If you focus on the way being healthy makes you feel and the benefits it gives you, this will help you to achieve real motivation to stay on track, plus a deeper sense of gratification for the results you will achieve. You will notice that the unhealthy choices you were making will lose their appeal, and foods that you once mindlessly ate will lose their attraction.

Allow healthy eating and exercise to become something you do that's a real gift of love to yourself, rather than being something that becomes a form of punishment and atonement for the unhealthy choices you've made previously. If you see them all as punishing yourself, you will naturally rebel against yourself and fall back into the unhealthy patterns of behaviour, so this switch in thinking is vital. Rather than obsessing over diets, instead let your focus be to feed your body in a way that helps you to feel your best and to ease the worries of poor health. Think of exercise as something that helps you to relieve stress, alleviate anxiety, release endorphins, and that helps you feel good. Look to also include meditation as part of the self-care of your body, for it will help you to get a clearer view of the bigger picture, foster a deeper connection to your emotions, and be more at peace. By moving how you see your body, you will help yourself to have a healthier relationship with both your health and your appearance.

I know it may sound like something you've heard a million times before, but the key to health and loving your body is balance: everything in moderation. Self-love doesn't equal living off lettuce leaves and water! In truth, if you deny yourself something, your mind will rebel and make you want it more. So, learning to love who you are isn't about not having the 'naughty' things like chocolate and cake. If you really want some, have it! But have a small portion rather than enough to feed a family. And, if you do eat something that isn't necessarily the healthiest option for you to choose, enjoy it and don't beat yourself up for eating it. I swear, guilt and shame add extra weight on to your body! Make sure that whatever you're going to treat yourself with is something you truly enjoy – there's nothing worse than wasting calories on something that doesn't taste that great. Once you have eaten it, move on. Don't let it send you on a downward spiral of self-sabotage where you use it as an excuse to pig out. Eat the 'naughty' thing and come back to balance. In that way, you'll be able to have a healthier and more balanced attitude towards food and your body.

Be careful too about the words you are using about your body; remember that you are always listening to yourself. It's incredibly difficult to foster an energy of self-love and acceptance for yourself if you're continuously engaging in a monologue of hatred. Whether you believe it or not, every single person upon this planet has some issue with their body... yes even him and her! That doesn't mean that you have to let those issues become your entire focus. Consider, would you say these words to your son/daughter/friend? Chances are you wouldn't, and if you did see an issue you would frame it in a way that is completely different to the way you talk to yourself. Inside your head, you are perfectly hateful, vile and cruel. But, if someone you loved needed to lose weight for example, you would approach them with a sense of love, compassion and support. Hating on yourself is going to do little but take you down a deep hole of loathing where all your hopes, dreams and aspirations seem completely out of reach.

*All I can be is me, whoever that is.'*
*– Bob Dylan*

A good way that I found to switch the conversation around was through the use of positive affirmations. Tell yourself every day, *'I am worthy and deserving of receiving good things into my life, and I accept myself unconditionally with love.'* Anytime you find the inner critic raising its nasty head, imagine a big black X through those words and say your affirmation again. Your mind will totally reject your affirmation at first, but that doesn't mean you shouldn't say it. Keep the focused dedication to changing your mindset towards yourself and you will find that your mind becomes more accepting of your new mode of thinking.

Ultimately, I stopped focusing on what was supposedly wrong with my body, and instead made my focus centre on my achievements, no matter how big or small. So, for example, rather than obsessing over what dress size I am or what the scales say, I started to celebrate all the amazing things my body can do. The fact that I walked over 11,000 steps in one day. Or that the dress that wouldn't go over my hips last year now fits me comfortably. Or even that I chose to eat fresh fruit over chocolate. These are big achievements and should be applauded! I focus every day on what good things I can do, and stop worrying so much about what I haven't done or can't do. It may sound like a small and insignificant thing to do, but actually it's incredibly important. Learning to love your body is all about how your mind views it. You have the power to change the inner conversation and focus. You can always decide to fall in love with your body, no matter what it looks like. And, when you do that, you'll naturally want to treat your body like the beautiful and sacred place it truly is.

# Step into Your Light

You may have an image of what you think loving yourself looks like.

An inner picture that sees you at your most confident, shining and happy self, where you're able to glide through life in a cloud of love. Any negativity will simply be deflected away from you, and every area of your life will seem to magically fall into place.

Sorry to burst your bubble, but this is real life, not a Disney film.

Loving yourself does bring in a greater sense of confidence, happiness, and self-worth. You will feel as though you are flowing through life with ease, and that things are magically falling into place for you.

But...

This book is not a magic lamp and I'm not a genie. Things are not going to simply transform in front of your eyes like magic just because you've wished them into being! I wish I could do that for you, but it's better to think of this book as your map to self-love, and me as your guide. I can point the way and explain things that crop up, but I can't zip you through it all at 100mph. From misery to the Promised Land faster than Usain Bolt! Besides (and you may not like this), the journey is just as important as the final destination... more so in fact.

If I had not experienced the years of low self-esteem and self-worth, I don't believe I would hold the same appreciation for loving myself now. If I had been born with truly unconditional and unshakeable love for myself, I doubt that I would have written this book. Everything happens for a reason in your life. Even before you started on this self-love journey, all of your life from the moment you were born till this very moment has added up to the place where you need to be right now.

This can be really hard to comprehend and accept for so many of us. It's easy when you look back at the wonderful times you've been through, but what about your challenges and tragedies? If you consider that everything happens for a reason, does this mean that these difficult times were somehow meant to be?

This can be a hard pill to swallow.

We all go through challenges and difficulties from time to time. Life has a nasty way of smacking us in the face when we are least expecting it. Some of them, we can see with the beauty of hindsight that they were meant to happen for us. Without them, we wouldn't be where we are now. Let me give you an example:

When my eldest son was born, it made me question what I was doing with my life. Before that point, I had been seemingly drifting from one thing to another, but there was little sense of direction or purpose. I didn't know who I was or what I wanted to do with my life, and I knew this had to change. When my son was eight months old, I left his father and moved back in with my parents. This gave me the perfect set-up to review and reflect on what I was doing, for I suddenly had the financial, physical and emotional support I needed to make big changes in my life. I wanted to give my son a good life where he would have the stability and means to have everything I wanted to provide for him. So, I knew it was time for me to go to university and get my degree; I was ready. Not only this, but I decided to go and train as a teacher afterwards too. I had always been passionate about books and reading, and I knew that helping to give children the same love of literature as I have would be amazing.

Four years of training, late nights and countless assignments. Rushing backwards and forwards between university and home. I made it a priority to come home every night to be with my son and worked when he had gone to bed. Yes, it was tiring and hard work but, with the loving help and support of my parents, I gained my qualifications, and was ready to enter the world of teaching.

You may have realised that I'm not a teacher now, so you can guess that my plan didn't exactly go to... plan.

My PGCE was in Post-Compulsory Education, which meant I was trained to work in colleges, but no jobs were coming my way in this sector. On an off chance, I applied to work at a secondary school.

I got the job.

Suddenly, three months after gaining my teaching qualification, I found myself standing in front of a class of thirty 12- and 13-year-olds in a high school; my heart beating so loudly I would've been a great addition to the school orchestra. Despite my nerves, my first few classes went well, and my romantic vision of being an amazing teacher gathered pace inside my imagination. I would be the kind of teacher that students talked about with fondness, helping to shape the adults they were becoming. I was making a positive difference, and it all felt very meant to be.

My second week of teaching didn't go so well.

A student stole my laptop.

I was physically threatened by three 15-year-olds for giving them a 20-minute detention.

I was sworn at more than I had ever been, or have been since.

It was dawning on me more and more that my romantic vision of teaching didn't match up to the reality. Far from Enid Blyton-esque tales of engaged students and an apple for teacher, in truth it was behavioural management, endless paperwork, and a bit of teaching thrown in for good measure. As a newly qualified teacher, I was truly thrown in at the deep end and I wasn't swimming to the surface. Each day I felt like I was drowning, and I knew that there was absolutely no way that I could stay there. In desperation, I secretly applied for other jobs, and I was offered a place at another school which started after Christmas. Convinced that maybe it was just the school that was the issue and that things would be better elsewhere, I quit my job and felt a growing sense of excited anticipation at this new challenge.

The new school was better. I didn't have the same level of bad behaviour as I had witnessed previously, although a good deal of my time still seemed to be spent dealing with behaviour management. But I still didn't feel fulfilled, satisfied or happy. I stayed in that role for 11 months, each day bringing a nagging feeling that I was on the wrong path.

Did I tell anyone about how I was feeling?

What do you think?

My parents had been unbelievably supportive during the four years of education I had put myself through in order to become a teacher. I truly believed that I couldn't tell them that I had made a mistake; I would be letting them down. So, I kept on plodding, hoping against hope that things would get better.

In the following November, I took myself to the doctors. I knew that I wasn't right, and I was starting to become really worried about myself. I was crying all the time, could barely sleep, and my appetite was all over the place – sometimes barely able to eat an apple all day, other days feeling ravenous and unable to satisfy my hunger. After giving me an assessment, the doctor told me I was on the verge of a nervous breakdown, and that I needed to leave teaching immediately. If I didn't, I would be in real danger of negatively impacting my mental health. At home, I sat in the bath, terrified of telling my mum and what she was going to say. In my tendency to overthink, I had built this up and was convinced that she was going to be both angry and disappointed with me. When she came into the bathroom, my mum took one look at me and asked me what was wrong.

*'I don't want to be a teacher anymore!'* I wailed, the dam bursting on my fearful sobs.

*'Then don't,'* my mum answered calmly.

*'But, I feel as though I've let you all down!'*

*'Don't be silly! We're proud of you no matter what! You've got your degree, and no one can take that off you. If you don't want to be a teacher, then don't be one.'*

Why am I telling you this?

For years, I felt really ashamed and guilty that I had quit teaching. I always saw it as a badge of failure and, despite my mum's reassurances, that I had let everyone down; especially myself. It felt like such a waste of time and energy when actually I could've been working on becoming the writer I always dreamed of being.

Recently, however, I have noticed a shift in my thinking. I now have the power of hindsight to see that my time as a teacher was not wasted, neither should I be ashamed that I walked away from it. First and foremost, I never quite fitted the teacher box. My personality is too big, my interests too varied, and my style too creative to fit inside the school structure. It's true too that teaching for me was a job and not a vocation. As a single parent, I couldn't get out of the door fast enough after the bell had gone so I could get home to my son. Although I always took work home with me, I still got glares and comments from some of the other teachers. I didn't have the same level of passion and dedication in me to put the role before anything or anyone else.

But, most importantly, I see now that teaching actually gave me lots of skills that I have been able to use since. As well as the fact that I have gone on to teach spiritual knowledge through my online courses and in-person workshops, I also gained:

- Active listening skills: the ability to give my full attention to people when they're speaking, taking time to understand the points they are making, asking questions, and not interrupting them.
- Coordination: adjusting plans and work in relation to the

needs of the individual, and working with others in a team for a common purpose.

- Critical thinking: using logic and reasoning to identify the strengths and weaknesses of alternative solutions and approaches to a problem.
- Judgement and decision making: considering the benefits of action to choose the most appropriate one to implement.
- Multitasking: being able to juggle multiple tasks and responsibilities whilst staying composed and meeting deadlines.
- Relationship management: conflict resolution, motivating, organising, establishing rapport, and troubleshooting.
- Speaking: talking to others to convey information clearly and effectively.
- Time management: managing my own time and that of others effectively.
- Writing: communicating effectively for the needs of the audience.

So, no, definitely nothing to be ashamed of, and certainly a period of my life that wasn't a waste of time. I can see now that my role as a teacher was absolutely meant to be, for it was all part of the journey to lead me to where I am now: writing, teaching and helping others. There'll be many moments in your own life that could be viewed through the same lens of hindsight to see that it was meant to be. When you look at your past objectively, you can see how all the pieces come together to put you where you are now. It's like looking at a tapestry from the back and seeing all the knots, tangles and twists, only to turn it over to a beautiful picture.

But, what about those situations that are less understandable? The ones that can't be so easily viewed through hindsight to see that they were meant to be? How are you supposed to accept the challenges you've been through when there's no easy answer as to why they have happened?

I'm not going to sit here and tell you that it's okay when people you love die, or children get hurt. It's not okay for abuse, pain, suffering or torment of any kind to occur, ever. In the notion of everything happens for a reason and the journey has helped you be where you are now, these tragedies don't seem to fit as neatly or as easily; and I'm not about to make them try. Over the many years of helping people, I have spoken to hundreds of people with heartbreaking stories, and it can all seem so senseless and unfair. This chapter is not about to condone what you have been through or explain it all away with a pretty bow on top. That would be unfair and disrespectful of me. If you have been (or are going) through something like this, my heart really does go out to you. Please know that, although it feels like it right now, you are not on your own. There are people and organisations out there specifically to help you; people who have been through similar things in their own lives and can support you. Do not suffer in silence or feel you have to get through things on your own. It's too much for one person to deal with.

What I will say is that these tragedies make you stronger than you ever thought possible. If you can get through them, the issues of everyday life suddenly seem smaller and less important. You find a courage and a resilience to keep moving forward; even when you don't have the first clue as to how you're managing it. Times like these do help you to realise the shortness and fragility of life. You see how important it is to make your life something that you can be proud of, and you may be more inclined to make dreams happen that you used to dismiss.

I'm not saying that everyone should go through a tragedy to get these benefits; neither am I saying that this is the only way to get them. I'm simply helping you to see that, even when you feel as though you will never understand why something happened to you and there seems to be no logical reason for it, know that you will come out stronger than you could ever realise. Even in the darkest cloud there is still the faintest glimmer of light, and this can be enough to help you move forward when all hope seems lost.

*You can't build joy on a feeling of self-loathing.*
– Ram Dass

In terms of learning to love yourself, your history is a fundamental part of the process, no matter how chequered or difficult it may have been. As I have mentioned before, it is important to make peace with it, but that doesn't mean you should then simply chuck it in the forget-it bucket and move on. Looking at your past helps you to understand yourself better, and to see the lessons you need to take to move forward to a space of real self-love.

The biggest lesson from the past for me and my own journey to self-love has been learning to accept myself for who I am and respecting myself. Every time I have found myself struggling with these two things, someone has shown up in my life to highlight what I'm doing wrong. Case in point, some friends I made whilst my eldest son was at primary school. Many mums find themselves chatting friendly to other mums in the playground, and it wasn't long before I became friends with some of them. Although this was many years before the real start of my self-love commitment, I see now that I was making attempts to be truer to who I was at that point and to be my authentic self. It was a difficult path for me to take at that point because I wasn't ready and didn't have all the knowledge and experience I needed to stay dedicated to maintaining these thoughts and beliefs. Consequently, it didn't take very much to push me back into self-loathing, and I would stay back in that dark place for longer periods of time.

What I noticed, however, was that, throughout this roller coaster of emotion, the relationship I had with these women was also incredibly unstable. Every time I tried to be true to myself, there would be little digs, passive-aggressive comments, and backhanded compliments. This was because they subconsciously saw me trying to shine brighter than them and it made them feel threatened and inadequate that they weren't doing the same. These women were my mirror, reflecting back at me the battle that was going on within myself. When I was flat, they would try and cheer me up, but when I was feeling on top of the world, they were quick to knock me off my pedestal.

It took me a long time to wise up to this fact. I mean *years*. In all that time, I may have complained about them at times in private, but I still believed they were my friends and relied on them to give me support. Thank goodness I woke up to what was going on! Let me tell you, sometimes you learn the lesson and then change the situation, but at times it happens in reverse, and this was exactly my experience with these women. As soon as I started to drift away from them and stopped relying on them so much, the relationship I had with myself also shifted. I'm not saying that moment was the answer to self-love (as you have seen), but it was a **huge** part in moving me closer to that space. I started to understand that I didn't need people in my life who were going to react in a toxic way every time I tried to be true to who I am, and that it was important to protect myself and my boundaries by avoiding getting into relationships like these again.

These are lessons from my past that I will always carry with me as I continue to move forward. The past is a valuable tool in this journey to loving yourself. It helps you to identify the times when you have not been giving yourself the love you deserve, how this has impacted on your life, and what has happened when you changed things. It's important to note that, if you are going to cast an eye over your shoulder and look at your past to see these lessons, you do so in a non-judgemental and loving way. It's no good to you in the slightest if you start to look at your past with guilt, shame and hatred for your choices back then. You did the best you could at the time. To really make effective use of looking back to get the lessons, do so with love for yourself, and understand that now you know better you can do better.

# Your Dreams Matter

As I have mentioned previously, I have held secret dreams of being a writer ever since I can remember. Dreams that I kept buried so well that I was even able to lie to myself. However, as with the birth of my eldest son, bringing new life into the world causes me to reflect on my life and the path I'm on. When I gave birth to my twins in 2012, I had exactly the same thing. Those writing dreams started to get louder in my heart; like an internal itch you can't scratch.

I finally decided to try and give these dreams the space they needed to manifest in 2013, and I started to write my first book. This was the spiritual novel *Chasing Rainbows*, and the whole experience stunned me from start to finish. I started off by thinking I may as well give it a go as I had nothing to lose but was totally full of doubt and anxiety as I picked up the pen to write my first draft.

*What if I wasn't good enough?*

*What if the dream I had carried all these years turned out to be nothing but a waste of time?*

Thank goodness I didn't quit at the first hurdle though for, as my words started to spill across the page, I found something: joy. All those years of trying to be someone I wasn't, having jobs that made me feel miserable, feeling like I didn't fit in – all of that faded away. The pure joy I got from writing was unlike anything else; it was as if my soul was covered in fairy lights. I was lit up from the inside and I couldn't stop smiling. I felt as though I had finally found *it*, my purpose in life. I had discovered why I am here.

*Until you value yourself, you won't value your time. Until you value your time, you will not do anything with it.*
*– M. Scott Peck*

So many people worry about their life purpose. They have a nagging sense that they are here for a reason, but they worry that they haven't figured out what it is and are wasting time doing something else. I get it, I used to feel exactly the same. However, many also believe that figuring out your purpose should be something that's complex; another worry to add to the list. The relief and surprise, when I share the secret that it's actually very simple. Finding your purpose is simply a matter of following your joy; the things that light you up. Those things that you love so much, you would do them for free if you had to. They are your life purpose, and it's all a case of following them until you find a way to blend your passion with a way of making money from it.

It's also worth noting that your life purpose isn't just one thing, neither is it fixed. Just as you are growing, learning, developing and shifting all the time, so too is your purpose. As you grow, it's perfectly feasible to consider the fact that the things that once lit you up now don't hold the same passion. That's okay! No one said you had to stay glued to one thing for the rest of your life. There's a whole world out there of people, places and experiences to explore, so allow the joy to guide you to where you need to be.

Back to the book.

I put so much time and energy into writing that book. Once I had finished, I prepared and sent it off to publishers. I had no agent, but I knew I had nothing to lose. I had to try and go as far as I could with this dream. If I didn't, I would regret it for the rest of my life.

The hardest part were the rejection letters; one back for everyone I sent out. I knew that rejection was part of the process – you couldn't be a creative person without being able to deal with it on some level. But, it was still hard to deal with; especially as I hadn't been privy to it before on this scale. Each one felt like a punch to the gut, winding me and painful as hell. Indeed, such was the onslaught that I nearly gave up altogether. I almost took is as a sign that this wasn't the right path for me; that I'd got it wrong.

Sometimes though, these obstacles and blocks aren't about being on the wrong path at all. Quite the opposite in fact. Sometimes it's more of a case of a test to see how badly we want our dreams to come true. A test of commitment and dedication to the goals. These rejection letters weren't a sign for me to give up, but more of a sign for me to change course. With grit and focus, I decided to self-publish my book instead.

Your dreams deserve to be given a chance too. Going for them is a huge testament to how much you're allowing self-love into your life. When you're in a place of hatred, criticism and fear about who you are, it's nearly impossible to make your dreams come true. How can you when you don't fully believe that you are capable of making them happen, or that you really deserve success anyway?

So, let me ask you this: what dreams are hiding themselves away in the depths of your soul? What secret wishes have been travelling around with you, waiting to be born? Are you ready to try and make them come true? Yes, it's scary. You may even still believe that you'll fail, but better to try and fail than live with a lifetime of regret and what ifs.

Start by getting really honest with yourself – what are the dreams you're carrying? Think back to your childhood, and remember what hobbies and interests used to bring you real joy back then. You may be surprised what you recall when you take some time to really think about it; there may be things you haven't thought about in years! What subjects did you enjoy at school? What did you want to be when you were a child? These are vital questions, for they will unlock the door to your dreams and, once you do that, then you can start to consider the very real possibility of whether these dreams are still viable and whether you want to start to make them come true.

Once you have identified what dreams you have been carrying with you, then you can start to decide whether you want to manifest them into reality. Don't panic – I'm not asking you to do this overnight! We all have obligations, bills and a lifestyle to meet. Dropping your current job in order to materialise your dreams may be suitable for some, but most of us will find it hard to be that cut and dried; but that's okay, you don't have to! When making any kind of big change, it's perfectly okay to transfer slowly by doing it in your spare time whilst maintaining your current job, and slowly tip the scales until you're ready to make the leap a permanent thing.

I hold my hands up: *Chasing Rainbows* didn't sell very many copies. Of course, I initially took this to mean that my dream leap had been unsuccessful. In my romantic imagination I envisioned my first book becoming a best-seller, and myself becoming an internationally renowned writer... hey, what can I say? I get carried away at times! But, just because it didn't sell by the million did not mean it was a failure by any stretch of the imagination. It showed me that I was more than capable of writing a book and publishing it. All those years of wondering and doubting, and I had done it. Rather than the lack of success being a reason to quit, it was a springboard to more; to try again, bigger and better than ever.

And that's exactly what I did! I wrote another book which I also self-published called *Little White Feathers*, and then I actually did get a publishing deal with my third book, *Happiness: Make Your Soul Smile*. Each step of the way was another rung on the ladder to making the dream everything it deserves to be. Doing it once wasn't the end... it was simply the beginning!

So, on this journey of self-love, are you ready to step bravely forward towards your dreams? Are you ready to make them come true?

You're ready.

You can do this.

And you so deserve to give it everything you've got!

# The Comparison Trap

What's wonderful about this journey to self-love is that you won't be on your own. The Internet and social media mean that it's now become easier than ever to connect with like-minded people and share experiences. You may not have the kind of understanding and supportive people around you in real life, but you can always find your tribe online. This can be a real source of comfort, understanding, knowledge, and give you a proper kick up the backside when you need it the most. Regardless of whether you have real life companions or people online, the effect is the same – they are a necessary part of your journey to loving yourself.

In truth, our loving friends and family are a key ingredient for self-love.

Why?

When moving from a place of self-hatred to love, it can be unbelievably difficult to make a start at times. We have spent a lifetime hating ourselves and are so conditioned in that mindset that making a significant shift can prove hard. At times like these, having the love of others can prove to be invaluable. They help us to see how wonderful we are, support us, can be our biggest cheerleaders, and love us with an energy that's like nothing else. In this way, they set us off on the right path, giving us the biggest dose of love when we need it the most.

I am so incredibly lucky and blessed to have the mum that I do. I appreciate the fact that not everyone has the same wonderful mother as I have. I don't tell you the details of my life to upset you or highlight what you may not have, and I'm sorry if you feel that way. My point is that we all have someone who truly loves us unconditionally and with a purity unlike any other. No matter if this love comes from a family member, a partner, a friend, or a child, we all have access to the gift that is the love of another. This person is worth their weight in gold; cherish them and know how blessed you truly are to have them in your life.

For all my championing of others, there's something else I need you to know. Something of a warning, I'm afraid. You see, as much as the love of others is a fundamental part to love ourselves, we can toss ourselves into the pit of comparison if we're not careful. Let me paint you a picture to show you what I mean:

When I started the journey to making my writing dreams come true, it was with tentative and nervous steps that I began. I was full of excitement to be finally taking the plunge, but the anxieties and issues that plagued my sense of worth didn't just magically disappear; in fact, they were louder than ever. All those years of fear that I wouldn't be good enough loomed large like never before. Each scratch of the pen on the paper made me feel sick, and there were many times when I doubted my ability to complete the book at all.

In an effort to make myself feel better I turned to social media. I follow a number of authors and spiritual teachers, and I told myself that seeing their posts would be inspiration for me. I would see where they were in their own careers and that would motivate me to give it all I had. But, in truth, looking at the people who I saw as my role models didn't give me that motivating fire. All it really did was tip me into a pit of comparison. I looked at writers like Doreen Virtue and Gabrielle Bernstein and felt that I was never going to match up to their successes. Rather than easing the fears that were rising up from my low self-esteem, the comparison habit was doing nothing but fuelling them.

What's crazy is the fact that I know now social media is a very narrow lens aperture through which to get a clear picture of someone's life. The majority of people only post the best versions of themselves; the successes, the joys, the good news. All the bad bits of their lives are filtered out, but this can leave others with a very warped view of the people they are following. Without that knowledge, you can believe that everyone else has the most incredible lives and you are the only one struggling. It can seriously mess with your head and have an impact on your life that you definitely wouldn't want to shout from the rooftops.

*The reward for conformity is that everyone likes you but yourself.*
*– Rita Mae Brown*

In my distorted view, I looked at the writers I admired and came to the conclusion that if I was going to be a successful author too then I needed to write like them. Yes, such was the low-level of my self-esteem that I had no confidence in my own voice at all. I had well and truly fallen into the comparison trap and was allowing it to make me into someone I didn't want to be. My first book *Chasing Rainbows* was not copied off anyone, but the style was. I was trying to write like the writers I admired, honestly believing this was the key to being successful myself. Reading this now makes me sad for the woman I once was, although I do know that the creative process is a journey where you grow and develop as you go along. As I've progressed in my writing, I have gained confidence in my own voice. I am now a lot less likely to allow myself to compare myself to others as I used to. I know now that everyone is dealing with their own issues, even if they don't share them on social media. Just because a person's life looks sparkly and amazing, doesn't mean that's exactly how it really is. The only person you should really compare yourself to is you, and you should always aim to be a better version of yourself.

We have all fallen victim to this at some point in our lives, whether you'd like to admit it or not, and it's something that has reared its ugly head in my life a few times; like with a good friend of mine a few years ago. She was also working in a spiritual field and was a writer to boot. And, she ended up getting an amazing job in London and having her book published, all within the space of a few weeks. I should have been over the moon for her, for she was my friend and I knew how much this meant to her. And, a large part of me was, but there was another darker side that was rising up when I looked at all of her excited posts on social media: envy and feeling like a failure in comparison. Looking at her success was making me feel that I should've been further along on my journey by now, and the fact that I wasn't must have meant that I wasn't as good as my friend. I fell into a sad little pity party for one and wore my victim hat for a long time.

> *The reason we struggle with insecurity is because we compare our behind-the-scenes with everyone else's highlight reel.*
> – Steve Furtick

The more I understood this, the more I saw that comparing my own life to anyone else's was crazy. It certainly wasn't going to help me love who I am! In fact, it was going to do little but pull me back down in low self-esteem. Plus, I didn't want to be one of those people who couldn't be genuinely happy for their friends' successes. I knew how hard my friend had worked to achieve what she did, and all the challenges she had been through. Focusing solely on these achievements was like looking at the tip of the iceberg without seeing the colossal chunk of ice hiding beneath the waves. The world has far too many critics as it is, and I didn't want to add to that number. I knew that if I was going to be really happy for the people I cared about to have the success and achievements they had been reaching for, then I needed to get my head out of the comparison game.

So, how did I do this, and how can you stop yourself falling into your own comparison trap?

First of all, it's wise to limit the amount of time you spend on social media. I know this is tough, believe me, but it will help you to feel better about yourself. Cut down slowly the amount of times you check it, and also how long you allow yourself to spend scrolling. So, if for example you're checking it several times a day at ten minutes a time, try to cut down to three times a day at five minutes a time. Oh, and definitely try to stay away from the people who trigger you to feel badly about yourself. You don't have to unfriend them, but you can hide their posts until you're feeling better about yourself. Trying to get yourself in a better head space whilst constantly seeing the people who are inadvertently making you feel worse about yourself is only going to lead you to a bigger state of anxiety and low self-esteem.

Take your attention away from the screen and back to things in the real world that truly matter. Spend quality time with your loved ones. No, it doesn't count if you're sitting next to someone but you're both on your phone or computers! There in body, but definitely not in spirit. Get outside in the fresh air, finish that book that's been sitting on your bedside table for weeks, or get some exercise. When you turn your attention to the things that are actually important, it'll give you less time to focus on what everyone else is supposedly doing. Plus, it'll give you a better understanding of yourself and your own life. This fresh perspective can help you take stock of what is actually important to you.

Finally, you can see your comparisons as signposts to what you need to focus on in your own life. What are your anxieties trying to tell you? Seeing my friend's success was motivation for me to work harder with my own projects, and to take leaps of faith that I may have been too scared to consider before; leaps that paid off for me. If there are people who you can't help but compare yourself to, ask yourself what is it about their lives that you feel jealous of. Can you do anything in your own life to move yourself closer to where you want to be? At the end of the day, you are not a victim and are totally in control of your own life. Loving yourself doesn't mean just walking around blowing kisses at your reflection; it means seeing where things are not as you would like them to be and taking control to shift them to a better place for you.

Having other people to walk alongside us on the journey of self-love is important in a way that cannot be stressed enough. They help us to see our light when we have our minds in darkness, support us when we're struggling, and celebrate every little success along the way. We are sociable creatures by nature, and learning to love ourselves is not exempt from that; no matter how much we view this work as personal and solitary. However, be mindful that any relationship you delve into is a healthy one that is going to help you feel better about yourself. You have enough to deal with in all of this without someone else knowingly or unknowingly adding to your internal struggle. For social media, there's an unfollow button too. If someone is bringing you down, it's okay to step away from them for your own self-care.

# Exercises to Love

There are many exercises we can engage in to help us bring more love for ourselves into our lives. Reading about my own experiences and lessons is one thing, but sometimes we need practical things that we can actually do ourselves to make our situation better. In this way, we feel as though we are in control of our destiny and happiness, which in turn will aid in us having a better opinion of ourselves.

I will go through some suggestions below, explain how they can help you, and how you can put them into practice:

## 1. Treat yourself

Whether it's a pamper day, buying yourself something you really want, enjoying a long bubble bath, or anything that makes you feel treated – engaging in this exercise is a great way to make yourself feel a bit more loved. We are always so keen to care for and look after others in our lives, but we're just as important as anyone else. We all go through so many stresses and pressures every day; it feels as though each moment of our day is taken up by various obligations. If you don't reward yourself regularly with treats, even if they're only small, then you can end up feeling resentful and burnt out. When we make the effort to give ourselves a treat, we are giving ourselves the message that we matter and are important too.

## 2. Listen to yourself

Loving yourself doesn't mean giving yourself what you want, but what you need. And figuring that out means taking the time to tune into yourself to listen. What is your body telling you right now? Where are you feeling tension or pain? These signs from your own body are easily ignored, but can actually give you vital clues as to what you need in any given moment. Modern society seems to practically encourage the glorification of busy, but you will find the journey much harder for yourself if you don't take the time you need to tune in and listen to yourself.

## 3. Care for yourself in the same way that you care for others

Are you at the top of your list? Or, is it more like you're at the bottom, or not even on the list at all? You can't get water from an empty well, which means you can't expect to be of any use to anyone if you're not looking after yourself. We're all so keen to love and care for others (which is wonderful), but you matter too. If you would give tough love to someone who isn't looking after themselves – give the same to yourself. If you would give a loved one some much-needed TLC – give it to yourself too. The more you can show yourself that your needs are important, the more you can shift your mindset to long-lasting positive changes.

## 4. Make a list of your good qualities

So many of us spend an unbelievable amount of time focusing solely on our supposed flaws. We put ourselves down at every given opportunity, and truly can be our own worst enemy. However, you are not just made up of flaws and negative parts, you know; no matter how much your mind tries to tell you this. You have so many good qualities – personal attributes, skills, appearance, and so much more. Write a list of all of your good qualities and stick it up somewhere prominent so you can read it every day. If you can't think of any, ask a trusted love one to help you. Their more objective viewpoint will help you to see yourself in a more positive light.

## 5. Forgive yourself

As we have previously seen, carrying around past anger, guilt and shame for your actions is going to do little but drag you down. It can stop you moving forward to the happiness you deserve, and can actually cause you to make decisions that prove very unhealthy for you in many ways. It's time to let it all go. Know that you did the best you could do at the time, and that carrying around unforgiveness towards yourself is not going to change anything that's already been and gone. Take the lessons and move forward to a brighter future for you!

## 6. Change your mental diet

For a long time, I was subjecting myself daily to newspapers, magazines and TV shows that were pulling me down. They were entirely focused on fear, judgements and negativity; and I wondered why I was ending up feeling so bad about myself and the world! Start by being mindful of what entertainment you're consuming on a daily basis. What are you reading, watching and listening to? How does it make you feel? Look to engage with more uplifting and positive content, for it'll make you feel so much better about yourself. I now read a lot of spiritual and self-help books, watch comedy and positive documentaries, and listen to music that puts the biggest smile on my face. Everything else has been abandoned or limited because I know it doesn't make me feel good.

## 7. Start each day by setting your intention

When you wake up in the morning, consider what you would like to focus on that day. Perhaps you want to set the intention to engage in more self-care that day, or perhaps you're going to focus on your assertiveness. Whatever your intention is for that day, by setting it first thing you will put that focus front and centre in your mind. In that way, you can help yourself to ensure it actually happens!

## 8. Monkey mind awareness

We all have a chattering monkey mind; a little gremlin that never shuts up... ever. Even when you're not consciously thinking of something, it still has the ticker tape of chatter running along the bottom of your mind, like some digital news channel. And, if you're not mindful of that voice, it could actually be your biggest block. It could be spewing hate and negativity into your head without you even being fully aware that it's happening! First of all, it's important to understand that you can't get rid of this altogether, no matter how much you want to. It's an innate part of your brain, but that doesn't mean it has to be in control. Awareness is key. Pay attention to your thoughts as a non-judgemental watcher. Don't judge yourself for the thoughts that rise up, for this will just bring more hate to the table. When you see what's going on within your monkey mind, then you can choose to replace those thoughts with ones that are more positive and loving for you.

## 9. Upgrade your physical diet

I'm not here to preach certain diets to you, but most of us eat mindlessly and make bad choices about food and drink. If we all ate when we were hungry, stopped when we were full, and aimed to have a balanced diet, then most of us wouldn't have the problems we do. The real key is a balanced diet that doesn't actually eliminate anything, for when you do you just want it more and can end up sabotaging yourself. If you want sugar and/ or fat, eat them. Just eat a reasonably sized portion, and make sure it's something that you're actually going to enjoy! Don't waste calories on food and drink that don't taste nice! Do seek to bring in more fruit, vegetables, wholegrain, lean meat, oily fish, and pulses. Oh, and drink 6–8 glasses of water a day too. These things aren't preachy, they do actually help you to feel better. When your diet is loaded with foods that are full saturated fat and sugar, or are ultra-processed and refined, it makes you feel sluggish and lethargic, plus you will negatively judge yourself for doing so. Make better choices and you will find that loving yourself becomes a lot easier.

## 10. Surround yourself with uplifting environments and clothes

What does your living environment look like? How about your wardrobe? If you are surrounded by mess, drab colours, and things that are both worn and tired, then you are going to find it hard to feel good about yourself. It's time to clean out the clutter! Get rid of anything that you don't use anymore or you've outgrown. Give it to charity if it's in good condition, or put it in the bin if it's seen better days. Then, think about the colour schemes that make you feel happy and either calm or energised (according to what you need). For me, I love bright colours, but you may prefer a more neutral pallet. Wear clothes that make you feel good, and you will shine so bright! In your home, clean up the dust, open the windows, and bring in things that reflect who you are. Your clothes and your home are an extension of you, and you need to ensure that they are making you feel good about yourself. Anything less than that isn't worth your time.

## 11. Celebrate your success

No matter how big or small, we all do things each day that we should be proud of. For some people, this can be as small as getting out of bed, for they may be dealing with emotional and mental issues that are clouding their thoughts in fear. If you wait for others to acknowledge and praise you for your successes, you could end up disappointed. They may not do it at all, or may not have the level of celebration that you were hoping for. So, stop waiting for others to give it to you. Celebrate yourself! Doing so means you are telling your mind that you are worthy of such praise, and it'll motivate you on to the next step. Whether you want to treat yourself or even throw yourself a party, send the message to your mind that you are incredible!

## 12. Create an accomplishment list and read it often

What have you achieved so far in your life? Whether it's your qualifications, life goals, awards, personal achievements, I guarantee you will surprise yourself when you take the time to think back over your life and list them all. We get so caught up in the stress of daily life and feeling as though we're not good enough that it can be pleasantly surprising to see just how much we have achieved to date. Writing this list and reading it often reminds you how capable, strong and amazing you are. It will give you a loving kick up the bum whenever you're feeling down on yourself.

## 13. Move your body

All forms of movement, exercise and play release endorphins and serotonin, which will definitely make you feel better about yourself. It's important the movement you do is something you enjoy so that you actually want to do it. Our bodies can do more than we give them credit for, and doing any form of exercise is going to help create a healthier relationship with it.

## 14. Learn something new

We get so stuck in our comfort zones, even though we know they aren't making us truly happy and fulfilled. When we take the time to stretch ourselves and learn something new, we are allowing ourselves to grow. No matter what it is or why you are choosing to do it (for work or just for fun), taking the time to learn something new can give you a very real sense of your abilities and increase your sense of worth. Even if you don't end up achieving top marks or being an expert at it, the fact that you have chosen to push yourself can give you a sense of achievement. You're doing more than someone who sits on their sofa and does nothing but wishful thinking! Step out of your comfort zone and surprise yourself with how fantastic you are!

## 15. Help others

Helping others is another sure-fire way to help raise your sense of love for yourself. When you're kind to others, no matter what form that takes, it also releases serotonin in your mind, which is a feel-good chemical. It's also released in the mind of the person you're helping. Giving back to others helps us to feel good about ourselves, which then spurs us on to help even more people. No matter how you choose to do it, seek to help others in a way that makes them feel good about themselves, and everyone wins!

## 16. Reverse any criticism

At times, our minds throw up really harsh judgements and negativity towards us. But, just because you think it, doesn't mean it's true or you have to accept it; you always have a choice. To counteract the criticisms, reverse them by immediately thinking three positive things about yourself. Sometimes, you may forget to do this, or the criticisms will be too loud. But, that's okay. Instead of hating on yourself for not reversing them (which will just make you feel worse), lovingly bring yourself back to the intention of positive change. You are on a lifelong journey, not a sprint. The worst thing you could do is give up on yourself, so it's important to keep trying.

## 17. Surround yourself with supportive and positive people

It's hard to be loving and positive towards yourself if you're surrounded with negative people. We are most like the five people we spend the most time with, for we assimilate with those around us. If you're with people who are negative towards you or themselves, it's going to make this journey incredibly hard. Set the intention to bring more positive people into your life, and consider whether you need to either remove or limit your time with any negative people you may have in your life. The positive people will inspire you and help you to love yourself.

## 18. Speak positive affirmations to yourself

Your mind believes what you consistently tell it. Affirmations can be a really good way to help you move your mind to a more positive and loving mindset. At first, your mind will reject them, but the more you commit to saying them aloud, the more you will notice that the way you feel about yourself will change for the better. Write them and stick them up on your mirror. Whenever you see them, commit to saying them aloud. Here are some suggestions to get you started:

*~ I have everything I need within myself.*
*~ I choose to stop apologising for who I am.*
*~ I have much to celebrate about myself and my life.*
*~ I believe in myself.*
*~ I love the person I am.*
*~ I am deserving of love, happiness and abundance.*
*~ I am not my mistakes.*
*~ The only approval I'll ever need is mine.*
*~ I accept myself unconditionally.*

Help yourself to move to a space of loving who you are. You have the power and everything you need within you to make it happen!

*You're always with yourself, so you might as well enjoy the company.*
*– Diane von Furstenberg*

# The Ultimate Declaration

In May 2017, my ex-husband finally moved out of the family home; 13 months after I had told him that I didn't love him anymore. Looking back at those months now, I am amazed that I managed to get through such an awful time. To live under the same roof as someone you are emotionally and mentally separated from is beyond difficult. During that time, I had mentioned the possibility of him moving out and explained that it was the only logical outcome to move us all forward (especially as he had to ensure that there is a roof over his children's heads until they are 18), but each time I did he became increasingly stubborn about the whole thing. For the sake of the children, I knew I had to keep my patience and bide my time. I knew he would eventually work out for himself that what I was saying was true and leave.

He did, of course, but it truly was the most hellish and challenging wait of my life. A time of living with someone who you don't speak to, and when you do you end up in an argument. Sleeping first back to back in the same bed, as your house is too small for a spare room, and then on the sofa was awful. I was with a man who is a chronic liar and emotional bully, and I ended up dealing with stress-related IBS and bad eczema. It was definitely tough.

When he finally moved out on 27th May 2017, relief flooded my body. It is said that you don't fully realise how much stress you've been under until it's gone, and this was certainly the case here. As the door clicked behind him, I suddenly found that I could breathe properly; as though a huge weight had been taken off my chest. As such, I knew it was vital to give myself some much-needed time to process what I had been through and heal from it. I had essentially been through a kind of trauma for the last seven years, and healing from that wasn't going to happen overnight.

Over the next few weeks, my internal dialogue flipped from anger, guilt, regret and a giddy sense of freedom. I spent hours replaying what had happened in my marriage, from initially meeting him in 2010 to him walking out seven years later. I had met him at one of the lowest points in my life, after the sudden death of my grandparents. The whole family were deep in grief, including myself. My parents couldn't stay in Rugby and had to move away. I wasn't ready to go, but had no clue how I was going to be able to stay on my own as a single mum with little money. I needed rescuing, and my ex-husband entered my life at the perfect time to do just that.

Our relationship was a whirlwind for a long time; I felt as though I was on a merry-go-round that I couldn't get off. We met April 2010, got engaged in the August, and moved in together the following month. The following October (on my 30th birthday no less), we got married, and a few weeks later I found out I was pregnant with the twins.

To say that my relationship to my ex-husband was crazy busy would be the understatement of a lifetime. For a long time, there were whispers in my soul that things weren't quite right between us but, because we were so busy bouncing from one thing to another, I ignored them and focused on the next thing for me to sort out. If I had taken the time to stop and go within, I wouldn't have been able to deny the doubts that were there, but I was worried on some level what might happen if I did. I still didn't believe that I could be on my own, especially when the twins were born. I didn't want to simply run away at the first sign of trouble; that wasn't what I had agreed to when I stood at the altar and said my vows of marriage. Despite my concerns, I desperately tried to make it work over and over again, but nothing I tried seemed to be the answer to making things better in the long run.

For, in truth, I knew that there were deep-rooted issues in our relationship. We weren't truly compatible and didn't have much in common at all. Despite his assurances that he would make an effort with my eldest son and even be a real dad to him, it also became more and more clear that nothing could be further from the truth. What actually happened was a system of low-level bullying, where my ex-husband continuously undermined him and got at him for little things that other people would barely notice. Consequently, my son ended up with his own low sense of self-esteem and worth, and that I could not ignore, or forgive my ex-husband for making my son feel that way. To watch my ex's poor behaviour toward me was one thing, but to see him leave an emotional and mental negative impact on my child was too much. That was when I knew I had to end the marriage, and it's a decision that I have not regretted since.

When my ex-husband moved out, I took my time to process everything that had gone on. As well as working through the pain and regret, I became increasingly aware that something else was rising up from the ashes too. This feeling can only be described as a line, shimmering in the darkness. At first, I didn't understand it and tried to make it fit a number of possible meanings as to what it may be. However, a few weeks later, whilst sitting in the bath, it suddenly hit me what this line meant: it was a symbolic sign for me to step up for myself.

Enough now.

Enough with accepting poor relationships; men who didn't treat me properly; being made to feel less than I am.

This relationship with my ex-husband was the last one, and it was time to draw a line under all of that time in my life. No more would I allow myself to enter a relationship that was less than I deserved. I knew that it was time for me to step up for myself and to finally accept the fact that I deserved better.

And that's when I made a decision – a choice to make the ultimate declaration of self-love... I would marry myself.

*Dare to love yourself as if you were a rainbow with gold at both ends.*

– Aberjhani

I had first heard about people marrying themselves a few years previously in a magazine article, and I had been intrigued. Known as sologamy, the practice is not legally binding, but that doesn't take away the symbolic importance of making that commitment to yourself. You can marry yourself if you are single, in a relationship, or even already married to someone else. It isn't about only having a relationship with yourself and no one else. It means that you promise to treat yourself with love, compassion and care no matter what. Although it may sound narcissistic to some, and even ridiculous to others, I knew it would be a true commitment to loving myself like no other, and the perfect ritual to mark this new beginning in my life where I put my own needs and care first.

Marrying yourself can be as elaborate or private a ceremony as you choose to make it. Some participants treat it like an actual wedding and spend a lot of money! For me though, this wasn't about anyone else. I didn't need guests, a fancy dress and a posh venue to mark this special moment in my life. This was about me and the relationship I have with myself. So, on 18th July 2017, that's exactly what I did.

Surrounded by candles as I sat in front of my full-length mirror, I faced my reflection. As some gentle meditation music played softly in the background, I took several deep breaths. Once again, I looked deep into my own eyes, seeing the light of my soul looking back at me. I poured love mentally into every area of my life, past, present and future. I forgave myself for all I had done, and I accepted myself exactly how I am; no judgements or criticisms against me in any way, shape or form. Surrounding myself in a large mental bubble of love, I softly said my vows to myself. I have never shared these with anyone, but I give them to you now:

*I vow to love myself for richer, for poorer, in sickness and in health, for better or worse for all of my life and all the lifetimes that are to come.*

*I vow to always be my best friend, cheerleader, and number one fan.*

*I vow to honour my calling and live my life as a work of art.*

*I vow to honour my spiritual path and create an amazing life whether I am legally married to another or not.*

*I vow to comfort myself during times of hopelessness, disillusionment, or any difficulty that arises.*

*I vow to live in the faith that my life is unfolding in mysterious divine perfection.*

*I vow to never settle or abandon myself in romantic partnerships ever again.*

*I vow to be my beloved always and in all ways.*

*And so it is!*

Afterwards, I shed a few tears. I cried for all of the pain I had experienced in the past; releasing the woman I once was. I cried with joy and faith for the bright and hopeful future that was still to come, knowing that things would be different from now on. This ritual was profound. It marked the moment where I drew a line under allowing myself to be treated poorly by others, and I stopped treating myself with unkindness and contempt. It was a profound and personal ceremony that I really cannot recommend enough for others to partake in, if you feel ready to engage with such a ritual in your own life. There is not a greater symbolic act of self-love that you can enter into, and you are definitely telling yourself that you are ready to give yourself all of the love, care and compassion that you need. It is not for everyone, but it is always there as the next step to self-love for you.

Marrying myself was the moment when all of the intentions

and work on loving myself suddenly kicked up a gear. I had taken an active step which showed my mind that this stuff wasn't just words to easily be ignored when it suited me; this was my life. Since then, I have found that the times when I am fully emerged in self-love last longer and are more profound. I do still have moments of doubt and criticism, of course. I'm still a human being with all the neuroses and issues that brings, but marrying myself has meant that I don't stay in those dark places for as long. The ritual has given me a benchmark, a foundation that has left me with more self-awareness. No matter what happens in my life, that love for myself is always there, bringing me back home to myself. I know that, no matter what, I will love, support and care for myself always. The love I hold towards myself is truly unconditional and ever-lasting.

# Don't Give Up

The journey to loving yourself is not a one-time thing. You won't start this on a Monday, and be totally an in-love with yourself sunbeam by Friday, but that's okay! The greatest and longest relationship you will ever have is the one you have with yourself, and it's a process that will therefore last a lifetime. Everyone has their own unique and personal experiences on this journey, but that's perfectly fine too. Like everything in life, what you go through may be completely different from what I have been through. This doesn't mean, however, that I'm right and you're wrong, nor that you're right and I'm wrong. The most important thing in all of this is that you hold the intention no matter what to keep trying to love yourself more, and that you never give up on yourself.

There are four stages of competence that we all move through when acquiring a new skill. These are:

1. Unconscious incompetence – this is where someone does not know how to do something and does not recognise the deficit. You may even deny the usefulness of the skill.
2. Conscious incompetence – a person still does not understand or know how to do something, but they now recognise the deficit in their life.
3. Conscious competence – a person understands or knows how to do something, but demonstrating the skill requires concentration. It may have to be broken down into manageable steps.
4. Unconscious competence – a person has had so much practice at a skill that it is now performed automatically and becomes almost second nature to them. It may even be able to be performed whilst executing another task

at the same time. The skill may be able to be taught to others, depending on how and when it was taught to them.

In terms of the self-love journey, for many years I was firmly rooted at stage 1. I didn't even know that loving yourself was a thing that was possible, or that others actually loved the person they were! Listening to people around me do little but complain about themselves and have real anxieties that they weren't good enough, I grew up believing on some level that no one really liked the person they were.

As I became a teenager and had greater understanding of the world, I moved to stage 2. I met people who did seem to hold a greater sense of compassion, love and acceptance for the person they were, I even saw the huge benefits these feelings had on a person's life, but I still found it hard to move to that space myself. I didn't even know where to begin, or if it was even possible for someone like me. On some level, I wished for it so badly, but didn't believe it could ever happen.

Two years ago, I moved to stage 3. I started to bring in practices that helped me create new beliefs about myself and start to give myself the much-needed love that I deserved. But, I was dealing with a lifetime of negative issues and thoughts that were not about to be torn down overnight. I was moving to a more loving space for myself, but it was a very conscious practice. It didn't come easily at all, and sometimes I would forget altogether and slip right back into those old habits of self-loathing. You would think that this stage is the easy one. After all, you have learnt the key issues and practices around self-love and you can see how it will be a massive benefit in your life, so it should be plain sailing from here on in. However, if you're not careful, you could find yourself becoming jaded and feeling like a failure the first time you slip back into those old thought patterns.

You have to remember that your negative ego has the job of wanting to keep you safe. It does this by trying to keep you where you are, even if that place is making you miserable. The status quo is knowable and predictable, so even when you know that you're moving to a happier future, it still comes with a sense of the scary unknown, and this sends the ego into a blind panic. It will do all it can to make you give up: criticise you, plunge you into fear, make you feel like you're not good enough, and so on. Anything to keep you stuck and safe. At stage 3 of learning to love yourself this means that the first time you fall back into your old beliefs and habits of hating yourself, the ego will jump all over it and use it as proof that you couldn't possibly love yourself, neither do you deserve to. And, consequently, you may find yourself giving up completely.

I urge you with everything I have not to! This stage may prove to be the most challenging, but it is here where the biggest lessons are gained. For it is here that you can see how strong, determined and capable you are. Stage 3 of the process of learning to love yourself can be particularly tricky, but it comes with valuable lessons that you wouldn't trade for the world. You just need to keep reminding yourself as to why you are on this path, and that you do deserve to keep moving towards love for yourself.

The final stage of learning to love yourself is unconscious competence. Am I at stage 4 yet? Occasionally. Sometimes, I'm so in the zone of love for myself that I don't have to think about it. It's become my natural state. However, I don't stay in that space. And, honestly, I don't think anyone can stay there all of the time. It's different with practical skills like driving a car – you will eventually get to a place where you can drive safely without having to consciously think about each part of the process all of the time. The skill becomes something that is more innate and automatic, and thus it flows so much easier for you. But, loving yourself is not a practical skill, it's a mental and emotional state. And, that means that it's in flux, just as you are all of the time.

No one stays in one emotional state constantly. You're not a robot! Even when you logically understand that one state is more preferable than another, life has a nasty habit of getting in the way. And, there's nothing wrong with having times when you feel fed up, angry, sad, or a bit icky with yourself. Everyone does, and that's part and parcel of what being a human being is all about. The difference is, as I said, that you have a greater sense of self-awareness, so you will find that you don't stay in a more 'negative' emotional state as long as you may have done before you began this journey to self-love. You can accept your emotions more and know that they are as much a part of you as the waves are a part of the ocean; they come and go. The underlying intention of loving yourself underpins it all, and having this foundation means you will always come back to this space at some point, rather than floundering around aimlessly in the dark.

*Loving yourself isn't vanity. It is sanity.*
– Katrina Mayer

We all have down days and times in our lives when things really don't go according to plan, but this is when you need to love yourself more. You need to show yourself true compassion, understanding and nurturing so that you can help yourself through the difficulties. It's not a time to give up on yourself and think you're not worth it – it's a time to love yourself fiercer than ever! Don't rely on those around you to do it for you. This is your life and it is your responsibility, no one else's. Yes, other people can make it easier for you to be happy, but they can't actually make you happy completely. We are all responsible for ourselves, no matter how good or bad things might be. You need to start treating yourself like your best friend and looking after yourself each and every day. In that way, you will be giving yourself the greatest love of all.

# Dear Me

I want to finish this book by writing a love letter to myself. You have been with me on this journey, and you have read about the many twists and turns my life has taken up to this point. There have been countless challenges, lessons, and tragedies for me to face and deal with. The path to both loving and accepting myself for who I really am may not have always been easy, but it has been the best decision I have ever made. And, as such I wanted to leave you with words of real love, in the hope that they will inspire you to think about your own journey and how much of your love you deserve to start giving to yourself. Stop waiting for some magical moment when you think you'll be more deserving to even think about it. There is no 'perfect' time to start, each moment that goes by in self-loathing is another one wasted. You can't get them back, but it's never too late to start. No matter how old you are, what your gender is, what you look like, where you're from, or what you do – you deserve to love yourself just as you are right now.

You can begin.

You deserve to begin.

Now is the time to come home to yourself.

*Dear Katie,*

*Oh, what a journey we have been on so far! As I have sat and written this book, I have thought about all the adventures we have been on together, and it's been really difficult at times to write them down. The pain, the heartache – some of it is still so raw after all this time. But, here we are. We have survived it all and come out stronger than ever before.*

*I used to wish that I had started my self-love journey earlier. I believed we had wasted years in loathing and self-hatred that could've been turned around to something more positive. How different things might have been if I had! But, here's the thing: everything happens for a reason. You wouldn't be the person you are now if you hadn't been through all of that pain. You wouldn't have the massive heart you do and the compassionate nature towards others if you hadn't have struggled yourself. Yes, it's been bloody hard at times, but the difficulties have left you with a greater sense of empathy and love towards others... and yourself.*

*I'm so happy that you can finally see how amazing you are! It took you long enough! Please don't worry yourself about those who say you're full of yourself and have got a big ego. Remember that you're only highlighting how poorly they feel about themselves, and they secretly wish they had the balls to go on their own journey to loving who they are. You've got nothing to apologise for. You spent years apologising, and 99.9% of the time there was nothing to say sorry for! All you have to do is keep holding your head up and being true to who you are. People don't like you? That's their problem. What matters is that you never lose sight of the love you have within your heart for yourself; that's the most important thing.*

*You are truly a phenomenal woman, Katie. Strong, loving, caring, and oh so bright. You are an amazing mum, loving daughter, and caring friend. You go out of your way to help thousands of people every single day, most of whom you'll never get to meet in person. You always say that you wish you had a magic wand so that you could make the whole world happy. Don't underestimate this as some silly little comment. It shows what a wonderful person you are!*

*Never settle for second best. You have done that time and time again, and it's brought you nothing but misery. Can we just take it as read that you've kissed enough frogs now?! Don't allow anyone to make you feel as though you're not good enough just for being you. Don't let anyone make you feel stupid, ugly or as though there is something wrong with you. Promise me that if you even get a whiff of that stuff you will run away from them as fast as your legs can carry you, okay?*

*Never stop following your dreams. Never compromise on the things that make you smile. No matter what, you deserve to be happy, and you don't need to settle for anything less than that. You're doing amazingly well on becoming the woman you always dreamed of being; don't stop now! You have big work to do, and you can achieve anything if you really want it bad enough. Remember: you didn't come this far to only come this far!*

*May the love you have for yourself never die.*

*May it continue to grow into the raging furnace it deserves to be!*

*You are amazing.*

*All my love, always and forever,*

*Me xx*

Take the time to write a love letter to yourself. Make sure it contains absolutely no judgements, criticisms, or hate of any kind. Encourage yourself, praise yourself, and give some much-needed love to the person you are. This exercise may seem a bit silly or pointless, but it's actually what your soul is crying out for. We spend so much time throwing negative thoughts and words at ourselves that we can be our biggest bully at times. And, let's face it, that mentality has hardly brought you much joy, has it? It's like giving a very long overdue hug to yourself, and I can't recommend it enough. Once you have done, stick it up somewhere you will see it every day to remind you of how wonderful you are. Self-love should never be a one-time thing.

# The Self-Love Pledge

Are you ready to commit to loving yourself? Ready to start this journey of giving yourself the love you both need and deserve?

I hope this book has shown you how important self-love is, and it has inspired you to make it a focus in your own life. It may not be the easiest journey for you to take, but it is one that will give you benefits beyond your wildest dreams. It's long overdue and, let's face it, hating on yourself has hardly brought you much happiness and peace, has it? It's time for a different mindset... a journey to come home to yourself.

Below is a self-love pledge. This document is not to be taken lightly, for it has the power to sprinkle magic over your whole life, and start to move you to a happier place. Anything that's not aligned with that will naturally start to fall away, or you may not want to be around certain people or situations. That's okay though, for you will make space for things and people who will help this self-love process continue.

Sound good?

When you're ready, read and sign the pledge below. Or, even better – copy it out and put it somewhere visible so you can keep yourself aligned with the love you deserve for yourself.

### Self-Love Pledge

My name is_____
and I am ready to start the journey to loving myself.

I accept myself now unconditionally. I love all of my flaws just as much as I do my talents.

I am perfect exactly as I am. I respect and honour my feelings, and I know they will always point me in the right direction to the callings of my soul.

I place my needs as the top priority in my life, and I listen to my body and what it needs in every given moment.

I practise radical forgiveness for my mistakes, and I know I continue to try my best and learn my lessons so I can move forward to happiness. Every action I take and decision I make is for my greater good.

I defend my boundaries and do all I can to make myself feel safe.

I promise myself that each day I will do something fun and enjoyable!

I ensure that I practise gratefulness, and show appreciation to myself for all I have accomplished so far. I make sure that I reward myself on a regular basis for everything I achieve, no matter how big or small.

I eat mindfully to ensure that my body receives the right nutrition that it needs, and I move my body on a daily basis.

I take time to do the things that bring me a real sense of joy and fulfilment.

I speak my truth always, no matter what.

I will only speak to myself with love and kindness.

My name is_____
and I promise to be the greatest love of my life from this moment on. This is the start of a lifelong romance, and the happiness I deserve.

Signed_____

Date_____

I'm so proud of you for taking the time to make this commitment to yourself; you are amazing! Let's all take this journey to love for the wonderful people we are, and cheer each other on every step of the way.

With love from my heart to yours, now and always xx

*Love is not something you have to earn, it's your birthright. Stop waiting for others to give it to you; step up to your own love for yourself.*
*– Katie Oman*

BOOKS

# O-BOOKS

# SPIRITUALITY

O is a symbol of the world, of oneness and unity; this eye represents knowledge and insight. We publish titles on general spirituality and living a spiritual life. We aim to inform and help you on your own journey in this life.

If you have enjoyed this book, why not tell other readers by posting a review on your preferred book site?

# Recent bestsellers from O-Books are:

## Heart of Tantric Sex
Diana Richardson
Revealing Eastern secrets of deep love and intimacy to Western couples.
Paperback: 978-1-90381-637-0 ebook: 978-1-84694-637-0

## Crystal Prescriptions
The A-Z guide to over 1,200 symptoms and their healing crystals
Judy Hall
The first in the popular series of six books, this handy little guide is packed as tight as a pill-bottle with crystal remedies for ailments.
Paperback: 978-1-90504-740-6 ebook: 978-1-84694-629-5

## Take Me To Truth
Undoing the Ego
Nouk Sanchez, Tomas Vieira
The best-selling step-by-step book on shedding the Ego, using the teachings of *A Course In Miracles*.
Paperback: 978-1-84694-050-7 ebook: 978-1-84694-654-7

## The 7 Myths about Love...Actually!
The journey from your HEAD to the HEART of your SOUL
Mike George
Smashes all the myths about LOVE.
Paperback: 978-1-84694-288-4 ebook: 978-1-84694-682-0

**The Holy Spirit's Interpretation of the New Testament**
A course in Understanding and Acceptance
Regina Dawn Akers
Following on from the strength of *A Course In Miracles*, NTI
teaches us how to experience the love and oneness of God.
Paperback: 978-1-84694-085-9 ebook: 978-1-78099-083-5


**The Message of A Course In Miracles**
A translation of the text in plain language
Elizabeth A. Cronkhite
A translation of *A Course in Miracles* into plain, everyday
language for anyone seeking inner peace. The companion
volume, *Practicing A Course In Miracles*, offers practical lessons
and mentoring.
Paperback: 978-1-84694-319-5 ebook: 978-1-84694-642-4


**Rising in Love**
My Wild and Crazy Ride to Here and Now, with Amma, the
Hugging Saint
Ram Das Batchelder
*Rising in Love* conveys an author's extraordinary journey of
spiritual awakening with the Guru, Amma.
Paperback: 978-1-78279-687-9 ebook: 978-1-78279-686-2


**Thinker's Guide to God**
Peter Vardy
An introduction to key issues in the philosophy of religion.
Paperback: 978-1-90381-622-6

## Your Simple Path
Find happiness in every step
Ian Tucker
A guide to helping us reconnect with what is really important
in our lives.
Paperback: 978-1-78279-349-6 ebook: 978-1-78279-348-9

## 365 Days of Wisdom
Daily Messages To Inspire You Through The Year
Dadi Janki
Daily messages which cool the mind, warm the heart and guide
you along your journey.
Paperback: 978-1-84694-863-3 ebook: 978-1-84694-864-0

## Body of Wisdom
Women's Spiritual Power and How it Serves
Hilary Hart
Bringing together the dreams and experiences of women across
the world with today's most visionary spiritual teachers.
Paperback: 978-1-78099-696-7 ebook: 978-1-78099-695-0

## Dying to Be Free
From Enforced Secrecy to Near Death to True Transformation
Hannah Robinson
After an unexpected accident and near-death experience,
Hannah Robinson found herself radically transforming her life,
while a remarkable new insight altered her relationship with
her father, a practising Catholic priest.
Paperback: 978-1-78535-254-6 ebook: 978-1-78535-255-3

## The Ecology of the Soul
A Manual of Peace, Power and Personal Growth for Real People
in the Real World
Aidan Walker
Balance your own inner Ecology of the Soul to regain your
natural state of peace, power and wellbeing.
Paperback: 978-1-78279-850-7 ebook: 978-1-78279-849-1

## Not I, Not other than I
The Life and Teachings of Russel Williams
Steve Taylor, Russel Williams
The miraculous life and inspiring teachings of one of the
World's greatest living Sages.
Paperback: 978-1-78279-729-6 ebook: 978-1-78279-728-9

## On the Other Side of Love
A Woman's Unconventional Journey Towards Wisdom
Muriel Maufroy
When life has lost all meaning, what do you do?
Paperback: 978-1-78535-281-2 ebook: 978-1-78535-282-9

## Practicing A Course In Miracles
A translation of the Workbook in plain language, with mentor's
notes
Elizabeth A. Cronkhite
The practical second and third volumes of The Plain-Language
*A Course In Miracles*.
Paperback: 978-1-84694-403-1 ebook: 978-1-78099-072-9

## Quantum Bliss
The Quantum Mechanics of Happiness, Abundance, and Health
George S. Mentz
*Quantum Bliss* is the breakthrough summary of success and spirituality secrets that customers have been waiting for.
Paperback: 978-1-78535-203-4 ebook: 978-1-78535-204-1


## The Upside Down Mountain
Mags MacKean
A must-read for anyone weary of chasing success and happiness – one woman's inspirational journey swapping the uphill slog for the downhill slope.
Paperback: 978-1-78535-171-6 ebook: 978-1-78535-172-3


## Your Personal Tuning Fork
The Endocrine System
Deborah Bates
Discover your body's health secret, the endocrine system, and 'twang' your way to sustainable health!
Paperback: 978-1-84694-503-8 ebook: 978-1-78099-697-4

Readers of ebooks can buy or view any of these bestsellers by clicking on the live link in the title. Most titles are published in paperback and as an ebook. Paperbacks are available in traditional bookshops. Both print and ebook formats are available online.

Find more titles and sign up to our readers' newsletter at
http://www.johnhuntpublishing.com/mind-body-spirit

Follow us on Facebook at https://www.facebook.com/OBooks/
and Twitter at https://twitter.com/obooks